ARTHUR SELDON: A LIFE FOR LIBERTY

Colin Robinson

ARTHUR SELDON:
A Life for Liberty

With contributions from
Martin Anderson, Stuart Waterhouse and
Basil Yamey

FOREWORD BY PATRICK MINFORD

PROFILE BOOKS

First published in Great Britain in 2009 by
Profile Books Ltd
3A Exmouth House
Pine Street
London ec1r 0jh
www.profilebooks.com

A CIP catalogue record for this book is available from the British Library.

ISBN 978 1 84668 249 0

Typeset in Bembo by MacGuru Ltd
info@macguru.org.uk

Printed and bound in Great Britain by
Clays, Bungay, Suffolk

The paper this book is printed on is certified by the © 1996 Forest Stewardship Council
A.C. (FSC). It is ancient-forest friendly. The printer holds FSC chain of custody SGS-COC-
2061

FSC
Mixed Sources
Product group from well-managed
forests and other controlled sources
Cert no. SGS-COC-2061
www.fsc.org
© 1996 Forest Stewardship Council

Lives of great men all remind us
We can make our lives sublime,
And, departing, leave behind us
Footprints on the sands of time.

from 'A Psalm of Life' (1832),
by Henry Wadsworth Longfellow (1807–82)

China will go capitalist.
Soviet Russia will not survive the century.
Labour as we know it will never rule again.

Arthur Seldon,
The Times, 6 August 1980

Contents

Illustrations

All photographs reproduced by courtesy of the Seldon family unless stated otherwise.

Between pages 44 and 45

Arthur with his adoptive parents, Eva and Marks Slaberdain.

Arthur outside his adoptive father's boot sale and repair shop in the East End of London.

Class 6 at the Dempsey Street Elementary School.

Arthur with his sister and three brothers, 1926/7.

Arthur on graduation with first class honours from the London School of Economics, 1937.

Arthur on wartime military service in Algiers, 1943/4.

Warrant Officer Seldon, 1943.

Arthur and Marjorie on their wedding day, 23 February 1948, outside Tonbridge Registry Office.

The wedding party.

Family group on the occasion of Arthur's nephew Ramsey Margolis's Bah Mitzvah in 1964.

Arthur and Marjorie's three sons, Michael, Peter and Anthony.

Arthur with members of the Mont Pelerin Society in the early 1980s *(courtesy of the MPS)*.

Arthur and Ralph Harris at the Institute of Economic Affairs in Eaton Place *(courtesy of the IEA)*.

Between pages 156 and 157

Arthur with Prime Minister Margaret Thatcher and Ralph Harris *(courtesy of the IEA)*.

Arthur with Lee Kuan Yew, Prime Minister of Singapore, 22 February 1980.

Ralph Harris, Arthur and Friedrich Hayek outside the Institute of Economic Affairs in Lord North Street, mid 1980s *(courtesy of the IEA)*.

Arthur and Marjorie outside Buckingham Palace after receiving his CBE on 30 November 1983.

Arthur with Martin Anderson at Lord North Street, mid 1990s.

Daniel Doron, director of the Israel Centre for Economic Social Progress, and Milton Friedman.

Arthur with Bill Hutt in the mid 1980s *(courtesy of the IEA)*.

Arthur at the ceremony nominating him as the first Honorary Fellow of the Mont Pelerin Society, September 1996 *(courtesy of the MPS)*.

Arthur with his brothers Sidney and Cecil in the mid 1980s.

Arthur and Marjorie on holiday in September 1981.

Arthur at his golden wedding anniversary party, 23 February 1998.

Arthur with Colin Robinson at the Institute of Economic Affairs 50th anniversary celebration at the Reform Club, June 2005.

Arthur Seldon, 1916–2005.

Acknowledgements

I would like to express my appreciation to Arthur Seldon's wife, Marjorie, and his sons, Anthony, Michael and Peter, for their invaluable assistance in the writing of this book. Peter Seldon has been particularly helpful in providing biographical material written by Chris Tame, finding documents, commenting on drafts, putting me in touch with people who could help and generally being the moving spirit behind the enterprise. My thanks are also due to Arthur's nephew, Philip Margolis (son of Arthur's brother, Cecil), who kindly supplied me with some of his father's autobiographical notes, and to John Blundell, Director General of the Institute of Economic Affairs, for his helpful comments on a draft. Finally, I would like to thank the three people who contributed their recollections of Arthur Seldon at various stages of his career – Martin Anderson, Stuart Waterhouse and Professor Basil Yamey.

The Arthur Seldon website

A website, www.arthurseldon.org, established by Matthew Seldon, Arthur's grandson (son of Peter Seldon), contains tributes, obituaries and other information about Arthur Seldon's life and work.

Foreword

Patrick Minford

Arthur Seldon was a fine economist who made a big contribution to economic policymaking. He did so by recognising, as an economist should, his own comparative advantage: to take ideas from the great liberal tradition of economics that he had understood so well as an LSE student, researcher and academic and educate non-economists in government, journalism and the other haunts of 'informed opinion'. I learnt from Colin Robinson's book, which I have read with fascination, that Arthur formed the opinion early on in his life that poor policies were the result of ignorance of good economics among our political classes. Thus there was a serious need for education of these classes and of the groups in society from which they emerged – the 'educated middle classes', as we might term them.

During his life he was consumed by an interest in ideas, and he followed the progress of economics over the post-war period as the profession dug deeper into theory and data to expose the ways in which markets dealt with all sorts of problems – public goods, monopoly, inequality, unemployment, public corruption and so much else – where government intervention was initially thought to be the only cure. As Editorial Director of the IEA he brought these ideas to the attention of the intelligent public, and made sure that those he collaborated with as authors explained them in pellucid prose, free of the technical jargon that can make economics so impenetrable to outsiders.

This biography movingly documents the struggles that Arthur had on this crusading journey. It is the story of a man who enjoyed none of the advantages in life that would be taken for granted by those middle classes he was to educate. The story of his childhood is the stuff of modern legend: he was the son of poor Jewish immigrants from Russia, orphaned by their tragic deaths in a flu epidemic and then adopted in the Jewish East End community with generous support from his uncle's family. When Arthur was eighteen, his adoptive mother was urged to send him to work, but she insisted he have the opportunity to go to university. What a might-have-been was that, to put beside all the other challenges of his youth – including being unable to take his grammar school entry exam through illness but going with a friend to persuade the headmaster to take them on anyway. He went to the LSE and studied under Hayek, Robbins, Coase and Plant; he got a First and then became Plant's research assistant. After a spell in the war on survey work he went into industry as an economist before becoming the IEA's Editorial Director at the age of 40 at its founding by Antony Fisher.

The rest of this book's story is of how he and Ralph Harris built up the IEA into a disseminator of those liberal economic ideas that over a 25-year period laid the foundation for the resurgence of liberal policy in the UK under Margaret Thatcher. This in turn led to the spread worldwide of these ideas among policymakers as they watched their success in action. This book tells us how the IEA editorial process functioned, the all-consuming hard work of finding and persuading the right economists to become authors, then working alongside them to turn their prose into the sort of English a classics-trained civil servant or columnist would understand both intellectually and viscerally.

Colin Robinson has assembled a variety of viewpoints to complement his own clear narrative: we see Arthur through the eyes of Marjorie, his immensely supportive wife of 57 years, his three boys, his working colleagues, and his friends. They all testify to his sense of duty and fun – indeed, the sheer pleasure of being with him. They contribute to a picture that I recognise from my own experience of this dear man: it is of a human being with incredible warmth and passion who bent the power of his personality and mind almost exclusively to the great cause of spreading the lessons of good, liberal, economics. Everyone who worked and lived with him, whether family, friends or colleagues, loved him while he did so.

Cardiff Business School
March 2009

Introduction

Arthur Seldon, who was born on 29 May 1916 and died on 11 October 2005 at the age of 89, was an economist and a man of ideas. Many people have ideas, but Seldon's were unusual in that not only were they thoroughly analysed and deeply felt, they were also clearly expressed, making them accessible to a wide range of people, including those without a technical training in economics. Seldon's conviction and the clarity with which his ideas were expressed made them remarkably influential. Indeed, they were powerful enough to bring about significant changes in the economic and social policies of governments in Britain and many overseas countries. As a result, they had a marked effect on the economies and societies of many countries and therefore on the lives of millions of people.

Seldon came from humble beginnings in the Jewish East End of London, but he rose to become one of the leaders of a small group of people who, in the last quarter of the twentieth century, brought about a radical shift in economic ideas and in the political consensus.[1] From 1945 to the late 1970s, governments in many countries, following the conventional wisdom of the day, pursued interventionist economic and social policies. In macro and micro policies alike, they tried to bypass markets, substituting political and bureaucratic action for what would otherwise have been voluntary agreements. Most influential economists of the time were followers of John Maynard Keynes and of the 'imperfect competition' school, both of which originated in Cambridge (England). The analyses and the conclusions of classical liberal economists, who had expounded the virtues of markets and explained the reasons why government actions to constrain market forces may reduce welfare, seemed all but forgotten.

But Arthur Seldon was determined to rescue from obscurity what he saw as the great truths of classical liberalism, absorbed by him during his student days at the London School of Economics and Political Science (LSE) in the 1930s. Starting in the most unpropitious circumstances of the late 1950s, when collectivist attitudes were deeply entrenched, he showed extraordinary vision and determination in helping to rediscover and to publicise the virtues of economic liberalism by producing practical evidence of its benefits and setting out policies that would allow it to be implemented.

One interesting and unusual feature of Seldon's career is that he was a radical who was simply not interested in engaging in the standard activity of many 'think tanks' – which is to try to persuade the government of the day to make marginal adjustments to existing policies. He wanted to overturn the political consensus rather than merely to modify it, and he took the long view that, no matter how hostile to liberalism the consensus might be at any point in time, in the end economic forces would prevail over political forces. In this view, he was influenced by, among others, the early-twentieth-century Austrian economist Eugen von Böhm-Bawerk, who, in a 1914 paper, argued that political power would eventually succumb to the economic law of the market.[2]

Economic liberalism was the only way forward, Seldon believed, if economic progress was to be made. Patient explanation of the benefits of liberalism, with rigorous attention to evidence, could bring forward the day when those benefits were generally recognised and could be realised. It was in such patient and detailed explanation that Seldon excelled and, working with a small number of like-minded people, he eventually achieved success. His principles would not allow him to become a lobbyist, seeking short-term fixes and trying directly to persuade politicians to change their ways. His view (in which he was influenced by Hayek) was that governments were more likely to change their ways as a consequence of a prior change in the climate of opinion, as reflected by 'intellectuals'. His writings and his editorial skills were major factors in moving the prevailing climate of opinion away from collectivism.

Seldon's written output, published in a seven-volume collection by Liberty Fund,[3] was very large. He wrote 28 books and monographs and about 230 articles. On its own, this written output would have made him an important figure in classical liberalism. But, as well as this considerable oeuvre, he was an extremely talented and effective editor, spending much of his working life, from the late 1950s onwards, in a fruitful partnership with Ralph Harris (later Lord Harris of High Cross) at the Institute of Economic Affairs (IEA). During this time, he edited about 350 books for the Institute.

As Harris has aptly described Seldon's role in the partnership, it was in the 'engine room'. 'Editor' does not adequately describe his contribution to the Institute. In his hands, the 'editing' function was an entrepreneurial activity. He was an activist, constantly engaged in thinking about what topics the Institute should address, finding authors and editing and improving their work. The Harris–Seldon partnership challenged a British establishment that was convinced of the virtues of collectivism and gradually but effectively converted it to an appreciation of the benefits of voluntary action and the use of market forces. It took about twenty-five years for a sufficient number of people to be converted to the idea that government policies could begin to change.

The Harris–Seldon approach was not so much direct persuasion of politicians and civil servants as a more general appeal to influential opinion, over the heads of politicians and their officials. The IEA, in Seldon's words, was the 'artillery' in the war of ideas, lobbing shells into enemy lines. It was not the 'infantry', engaged in grappling with the enemy at close quarters: the grappling was left to other organisations closer to party politics, such as the Centre for Policy Studies.[4] Harris and Seldon set out an alternative agenda of liberalism which, after many years in which the failures of collectivism were increasingly demonstrated, eventually came to be accepted. The British government elected in 1979, generally (though not entirely) sympathetic to market liberalism, sensed that opinion had changed sufficiently that it could move away from the interventionism typical of earlier post-war years and adopt, if not as quickly or as effectively as Seldon would have wished, an approach in which government began to withdraw and market forces were given a prominent role. The governments of many other countries followed. The conversion to liberalism is as yet incomplete, particularly in attitudes towards the 'welfare state'. But the distance that has been travelled is manifested in the political platforms of the major political parties in Britain and other developed countries, which are fundamentally different from those of 30 years ago and have moved a long way towards the liberal market agenda originally set by Arthur Seldon and Ralph Harris.

Difficult as it is to trace the origin of the ideas of such an influential person as Arthur Seldon, it seems likely that the seeds of his liberal market views were sown in his early years, when he was brought up in the working-class East End of London in a Jewish family that believed in hard work as a means of coping with adversity and in a community where people were expected to help themselves but where that community gave help to those with temporary problems and the disadvantaged. This voluntary system of welfare clearly made an impression on Seldon and influenced his views about government welfare provision. His ideas about the roles of markets and governments were then stimulated and developed at the LSE in the mid and late 1930s, where he was influenced by some of the great economists of the period. Seldon was always conscious of his debt to Friedrich Hayek, Lionel Robbins, Arnold Plant and his other teachers at the LSE and, for ever after, he acknowledged that debt and tried to build on the work of his LSE teachers. One of his missions was to explain their work and its implications to a circle much wider than technically trained economists.

The main focus of this book is Arthur Seldon's working life and the intellectual contribution he made. They are discussed in Parts II and IV. The book is intended to be self-contained but it can also be treated as a companion volume to *The Collected Works of Arthur Seldon*, which contains Seldon's major works and commentaries on them. *The Collected Works*, to which there are frequent references throughout this book,[5] contains some biographical material in the introductions to each of its seven volumes. But this book is an attempt to assemble a more complete picture of Arthur Seldon and the contribution he made to economic ideas and economic policymaking.

An essential preliminary to assessing that contribution is to describe his formative years, including his education, which were followed by war service in the British army. Part I is therefore concerned with the period from his birth in 1916 to World War II (1939–45) and its immediate aftermath. Fortunately, there is an account of this period which stems mainly from Seldon himself in an unpublished draft about Seldon's early life prepared by the late Dr Chris Tame.[6] In the spring of 2000, Seldon commissioned Tame to write his biography and, to that end, Tame went on regular weekend visits to the Seldons at their home near Sevenoaks in Kent and conducted interviews with Seldon and his wife, Marjorie, about his life, his ideas and the influences on him. Tame died in March 2006, having drafted only the initial part of the proposed biography. Nevertheless, his draft, based mainly on his conversations with Seldon, which covers the period from 1916 to the late 1940s, gives an insight into how Seldon saw his early life and provides an interpretation of that period by a sympathetic observer, who held to classical liberal principles and shared many of Seldon's ideas and values. The title of this volume, *A Life for Liberty*, is the one that Tame agreed with Seldon for the biography he had begun to write.

Tame intended to produce an 'authorised biography' and, as he wrote in the introductory remarks to his draft, '... I have been given full access to all the available papers and many hours of frank interviews with both Arthur and Marjorie Seldon and many of their friends and colleagues'. The material in Tame's draft of the first part of his proposed biography forms one of the principal foundations of Chapter 1 of Part I below. Chapter 1 also owes a great deal to conversations and correspondence with members of the Seldon family, particularly Marjorie and Peter, about their recollections of Arthur, and to some unpublished autobiographical notes by Arthur's brother, Cecil, which were supplied to me by Philip Margolis, Cecil's son. Part I also includes two brief papers – the first from Arthur's friend and contemporary at the LSE, Stuart Waterhouse, and the second from another close friend from the LSE, Professor Basil Yamey – both of which are helpful in understanding Seldon's life in the 1930s, 1940s and 1950s, before he began work at the IEA. To complete Part I, Chapter 3 considers some of the influences on Seldon's work from his upbringing in the Jewish community of the East End of London.

In a book such as this, there is a danger of failing to reveal what Arthur Seldon was like as a man. To give some idea of Arthur's wider qualities, in Part III there is a short chapter on the Seldons' family life, based mainly on the recollections of Arthur's three sons, followed by a chapter about working with Arthur by Martin Anderson, who was with him at the IEA for many years. These contributions give a glimpse of the warm and helpful person who was such a good husband to Marjorie and father to his children, and who is remembered with such affection by his friends and colleagues (including many authors who benefited from his always careful and penetrating criticism of their efforts).

Arthur could be sharply critical of collectivist views, or indeed of the views of classical liberals if they were not carefully and clearly expressed. He expected high standards of others. But he was always genial and tolerant in his dealings with people, whatever their views about the issues that concerned him. One symbol of the affection in which Arthur was held remains in the form of a book that was produced on his 80th birthday in 1996. The book, *Letters on a Birthday*,[7] which was Marjorie's idea, contains letters from many of his friends, including numerous eminent people who had written for the IEA (and therefore felt the weight of Arthur's editing skills) or otherwise worked with Arthur during his long career.[8] It says much about Arthur's personal qualities that so many people responded to the invitation to contribute, demonstrating the warmth of their feelings and their admiration for Arthur in the messages they sent. Many of them had attended the 'parties for non-conformists' that Arthur and Marjorie organised at the Thatched Cottage in Godden Green. Subversive views about the conventional wisdom, and radical ideas for change, were the common topics of conversations at those occasions, which are still remembered with pleasure by those lucky enough to have been there.

PART I

THE FORMATIVE YEARS

1

Arthur Seldon's early years

Childhood and school, 1916–34

Arthur Seldon was born Abraham Margolis on 29 May 1916, the son of Masha and Pinchas Margolis, who had arrived in the East End of London as Jewish immigrants from Russia. The date of their arrival is somewhat uncertain, but it was in either 1903 or 1904, so they had been settled in London for some years before Arthur's birth. Arthur was not born at home, as many children were in those days. According to his brother Cecil,[1] his mother, Masha, experienced some health complications which meant she went into Mrs Levy's Maternity Home in the Aldgate area, probably in Petticoat Lane, for the birth.

Masha and Pinchas Margolis had married in Kiev (in what is now Ukraine), Pinchas having been born in the nearby village of Perioslov. There does not appear to be any information about Masha's place of birth but it was presumably in the region of Kiev. Masha and Pinchas joined the thousands of Jews who emigrated to Britain from Russia and Poland in the late nineteenth and early twentieth centuries, escaping from persecution, and became part of the large Jewish community that had become established in London's East End. This East End community, though poor, developed norms of self-help and voluntary aid, which were described in some detail in Charles Booth's survey of life and labour in London (Chapter 3 below), and which turned out to be an important influence on Arthur Seldon as he grew up.

The Margolis family was evidently very poor. Pinchas was employed in a cap-making workshop which, Cecil Margolis says, was named Goldstein and located in the Commercial Road. The Margolis home was originally at 12 St Marks Street, near Aldgate, an area where many Jews settled, but in 1913 the family moved to 74 Bedford Street, Stepney.[2] Masha and Pinchas had four children before Arthur, their last: Jack (born 1906), Cecil (born 1908), Bess (born 1910) and Sidney (born 1911). Like Arthur, Cecil and Sidney changed their first names – from Susman and Solly, respectively – though they retained the Margolis surname. Two other members of Masha's family, her brothers, Ben and Morris, also fled from Russia and arrived in the East End.[3]

The two brothers turned out to be important benefactors as far as Arthur and the other Margolis children were concerned. In 1918, when the Spanish flu swept through Europe, Masha and Pinchas died in the epidemic, only a week apart. Ben and Morris, who seem to have been fairly poor themselves, nevertheless took responsibility for the five orphans. The younger brother, Ben, and his wife Rosie, took Bess into their own home in Mile End Road from which they ran a small women's tailoring business. Jack, Cecil and Sidney, the three older brothers, were placed in Norwood Jewish Orphanage in Surrey. Arthur, however, then two years old, was found foster parents, who were given financial support by Ben and Morris. According to Cecil Margolis, Arthur had several foster parents, none of whom proved satisfactory to the uncles, and it was fortunate therefore that another young Jewish immigrant couple, who were childless, Eva and Marks Slaberdain (or Slabadain), offered to adopt Arthur. The Agreement of Adoption survives and is reproduced on pages 150–51, signed by Masha's brothers, Morris and Benjamin (Uncle Ben) Kopeloff.

Marks Slaberdain was a self-employed boot repairer, working

from his home (154 Oxford Street, Commercial Road, Stepney, according to the Agreement of Adoption), which was typical in many ways of the 'respectable working class' of that time, especially in the Jewish East End. Hard work and help for other members of the community were accepted norms of behaviour and education was respected (see Chapter 3). Indeed, it is significant that Seldon's adoption agreement specifies that his adoptive parents promise to give him a good education. Marks Slaberdain 'undertakes at his own expense to give the infant a thoroughly good education suitable to his own rank in life', as well as 'properly to maintain the infant and at all times during his infancy to furnish him with all things necessary or suitable for a person of his age in such rank as aforesaid'.

Chris Tame's notes record that Seldon told him that the Slaberdains provided a secure and loving home for him, probably little different in class, character and affection from that of his natural parents.

> Amongst his earliest memories Seldon remembers that he attended synagogue and that his step-parents sang in the choir, even receiving some financial remuneration for this. But, although religiously orthodox, the home does not seem to have been at the dour end of the spectrum of orthodoxy.

Tame goes on:

> The family was not well-off, but nor was it subject to the soul-grinding poverty of the lower levels of the working class. 'Comfortable, reputable, respectable' were the words that came to Seldon's mind when speaking of his life at this time. The social pathologies of drunkenness, divorce or wife-beating were absent. Although the traditional Jewish respect for learning and for culture was certainly shared by the Slaberdains, it was not a bookish home. They did not read English, and Seldon recalls having no

great access to books other than those at school. His
reading during his childhood was confined to school
textbooks and the popular boys' comics of the day such
as *Magnet* and *Tiger Tim*. However, on earnings of only
£3 per week – from which 10 shillings had to be
deducted for rent – his adoptive parents paid 2 shillings a
week for private violin lessons. The Slaberdains rented
out two rooms in their Oxford Street house to tenants to
supplement the family income. The young Arthur helped
his father sell second-hand boots in Whitechapel market
on Saturdays as well as in minor cobbling tasks, and also
earned money doing other odd jobs and by singing in
the local synagogue.

The first known picture of Arthur Seldon, reproduced on
the back cover, is taken outside the Oxford Street house, showing
boots in the window.

Although Arthur had been separated from his siblings very
early in life, he continued to have contact with them, apparently
assuming, or being led to believe, that they were his cousins. It
was not until he was eleven, in 1927, that he discovered that he
was adopted. The story is that he found out from his brother,
Jack, who had left the orphanage at fourteen and had gone into
employment with a greetings-card business. Jack, by then 21,
was visiting the Slaberdains and wrote 'Arthur is my brother'
with a stick in some dirt in the street. Discovering about his
adoption in this unusual and startling way does not seem to have
altered Arthur Seldon's loving relationship with Mrs Slaberdain.
It may have had some effects, however: Arthur's wife, Marjorie,
believes that the stammer from which Arthur suffered for the
rest of his life may have originated from the shock of this event.
Seldon told Chris Tame that Jack had always made him feel
special, taking him for bus and tram rides and giving him small
coins, but he had no inkling that they were brothers.

The Slaberdain home seems to have provided a supportive
environment during Seldon's schooling, despite the absence of

books. Arthur, who was good at mathematics and especially
enjoyed history, attended Dempsey Street Elementary School,
the local state primary school, from the age of five until he was
ten. In 1925 he was due to take the qualifying examination that
selected pupils for further education. He was ill at the time of
the examination, however, and therefore missed it. Consequently,
he – along with one of his friends – was offered a place only at
a local secondary school, rather than, as had been expected, at
the local grammar school, the Sir Henry Raine's School in
Arbour Square off the Commercial Road. Undaunted by this
apparent setback, and demonstrating an early capacity for self-
help, Arthur and this friend[4] conceived the adventurous plan of
going direct to the school's headmaster, Mr W. A. Wilkinson
Dagger, to plead their case. Their unannounced visit succeeded,
and the headmaster, who was clearly impressed by the boys'
manifest intelligence, the examples they had brought of their
schoolwork, and their initiative, promised to do whatever was
necessary to ensure their admission. Marjorie Seldon recalls that
Arthur told her that the headmaster's words were 'By hook or
by crook, you shall come to this school'. She recalls also that Sir
Henry Raine's was a charity school and had a number of free
places for deserving cases, which it could allocate without refer-
ence to the County Education Committee. Thus the headmaster had more freedom of action than he would have had in
many schools, and it seems that Arthur and his friend received
such free places.

According to Chris Tame, Seldon did not have any particular
interest in politics in his early years.

> His adoptive parents were typical of those of their class in
> supporting the Labour Party, but were neither overly
> concerned with, nor extreme, in their politics. Seldon's
> own first political memory was, at the age of eight,
> cheering John Scurr, the local Labour Party candidate for
> the constituency of Stepney in the 1924 General
> Election.[5] Insofar as he had any conscious political

orientation during his childhood, it was at this time a mild form of support for the Labour Party, which seemed to have the interests of ordinary people closer to its heart than anyone else.

During his time at the Sir Henry Raine's School, however, Arthur Seldon's views on economic and political issues began to form. He told Tame the following about his schooldays.

It was at the Sir Henry Raine's School that Arthur recalls the first glimmerings of libertarian ideas. In 1932, in his 6th form, at the age of sixteen, he recalls clearly the lessons of his history master, E. J. Hayward. Hayward was undoubtedly a classical liberal, and, although not heavy-handed or politically explicit in his teaching, hearing about the detrimental effects of the guild system of the Middle Ages and of the statist policies of mercantilism began to spark in the young Seldon doubts about the wisdom of the manifestly similar statism that had come to predominate in his own time. 'Whitehall knows best', the necessity of radical 'closed-shop' trade unionism and strikes, the alleged virtues of scientific 'planning' of social and economic life – these were the predominant political sentiments of the time, not only in the Labour Party and the general socialist and communist movements, but in the Conservative Party, in those who advocated national socialism and the Fascist corporate state, and even in large sections of so-called 'neo-liberal' thought. The similarities between what at the time even Keynes called, approvingly, the 'new mercantilism' could not – and did not – escape a bright and enquiring mind. As Seldon put it later, Hayward recognised a budding kindred liberal spirit in the young Seldon, and lent him some of his own study notes.

The school's economics teacher, J. M. Bence, a Fabian social-ist, seemed less convincing in contrast – although he did alert the young Seldon to the dangers of the rise of fascism and national socialism, and its British manifestation in the ex-Labour Party politician and demagogue Sir Oswald Mosley, whose provocations included marches through Jewish areas of the East End. Bence's lessons were not, however, biased, and for the first time Seldon heard the name of a bright young economist then at the London School of Economics – Friedrich Hayek.

Clear evidence of how classical liberal views were forming in the young Seldon before he left school is provided by an essay that he wrote before he went to university, which fortunately survives. Discovered among his papers by his son, Peter, it is entitled 'Some reflections on the science of political economy' (by A. Slaberdain). It was written in January 1934 when he was seventeen and still at school. Comments by his teacher (presumably his economics teacher) are written in the margins, with a general remark at the end, of the type essay-markers are prone to make – 'well worth reading'.

The essay begins with a statement of the young Seldon's view that many of the world's problems arise because so many people do not understand economics. That is the reason, he says, why misguided policies such as restrictions on trade are advocated. Politicians, in particular, should beware of imposing trade restrictions that will benefit sectional interests: they should be working for the benefit of the whole community, which means trade should be free. Everyone should learn basic economic principles, according to Seldon, so such gross errors will not be made.

In the latter part of his essay, Seldon enters into the debate about a 'very vexed question of the day – that of "Laissez-Faire versus Economic Planning"'. He says that, despite the view of many well-informed people that the days of laissez-faire, of liberalism and individualism, are past, 'I believe that Laissez-Faire is still the best policy for the world' and that 'State tampering with prices and interference in any industries but natural monopolies … must lead to chaotic results'. He ends by saying that he started out in life as a true patriot, then became a 'rabid fiery socialist', before concluding his essay with the following words:

I find now that my opinions were based on sentiment and snobbishness – on the observation of the conditions under which some of the less fortunate members of society lived. The study of economics has not only exposed the fallacy of the absurd opinions which I once held, but has also even prejudiced me against my former political friends. The study of economics has been the cause of my moving to the Right. Will I change again? I wonder …

The first and last pages of Seldon's essay are reproduced on pages 154–5.

By the time he went to university, therefore, Seldon already had opinions about economic issues which had latterly moved away from socialism to market liberalism. Despite his comment at the end of the essay, he never moved back.

Before this time, however, there had been another personal tragedy. When Seldon was ten, in 1926, his adoptive father, Marks Slaberdain, died at the age of 47. As Seldon recounts,[6] the financial impact of his father's death was considerably reduced by a death benefits payment received by Eva Slaberdain (Eva Marks, as she came to be called, using her husband's first name[7]) from her husband's trade-related friendly society. She received £100, a considerable sum at the time, which, in addition to her own earnings from selling boots and lisle stockings from the front room of her home and some help from the Jewish Board of Guardians,[8] enabled the family to live relatively comfortably for a number of years. The young Seldon recognised the lessons from this episode. Even a relatively poor man could, it seems, provided he lived responsibly and frugally, make provision for the welfare of his family after his own death. Tame mentions an interview with Seldon in which he commented that

the experience of family cohesion may be where I derived my later philosophic resentment of the welfare state for usurping the role of parents and weakening the bonds of family … [and] inspired my present interest in the early self-help of the working classes in the nineteenth century that was almost destroyed by the welfare state.

Then, in April 1931, when Arthur was nearly fifteen, Eva Marks remarried. (The marriage certificate is reproduced on pages 152–3.) Her new husband, Simon Finkelstein, was a master tailor and better off than her previous husband. The family moved to Finkelstein's home in the more middle-class area of Stapleton Road, Stroud Green, in North London,[9] where they had the luxury of a proper bathroom and an inside toilet. Seldon continued to attend the Sir Henry Raine's School, however, travelling by tram from his new home.

The London School of Economics, 1934–7

In 1934 Seldon won a state scholarship worth £80 per year to attend a university of his choice, and he decided to go to the London School of Economics. His Uncle Ben's wife is reputed to have urged on Arthur's mother that he should go out to work, to contribute to the family income, rather than going to university, but Eva Marks retorted that 'My Arthur will have all his education'. Marjorie Seldon recalls that Arthur remembered for the rest of his life how much he owed to his mother's insistence that he take up his university place. He supported his mother for the rest of her life, including her last few years when she was a resident in the Jewish Home for the Aged, where she paid her way (unlike most of the residents) with her weekly cash from Arthur. Seldon's time at the LSE was one of the principal forces that shaped his later life. He told Chris Tame that his 'intellectual birth' occurred at the LSE and that 'My conscious life of social conditions, of poverty, of inequality starts there'.

In the sixth form, Seldon had studied history, geography, German, science and economics. But, as the essay mentioned earlier makes clear, it was economics which excited him. He thought everybody should learn the elements of economics to avoid their making the mistakes in policy (such as imposing trade restrictions) which he saw all around him. According to Chris Tame, Seldon told him that 'he was excited by economics as a tool for both understanding and improving the real world'. But Seldon said also that his decision to study economics was driven by his wish to make a living and to escape poverty. He therefore selected a broad-based degree course with a practical orientation, the Bachelor of Commerce in the economics of industry, which seemed to offer good prospects of employment after graduation.

As explained above, the seeds of classical liberal ideas had already been sown in Seldon's mind before he left school. The influence of the LSE economists reinforced, both with theory and with evidence, views that Arthur Seldon was already forming, as he brought to bear on his own experience of life in the Jewish East End of London (see Chapter 3) his early reading of economics. An important part of that early reading seems to have been his assigned textbook at school, Edwin Cannan's *Wealth: A Brief Examination of the Cause of Economic Welfare*, which acquainted Seldon with the ideas of one of the LSE's leading economists.

Edwin Cannan had become the LSE's first Chairman of Economics in 1907 and remained so until 1926. As Seldon wrote in an appreciation of Cannan published in 1996, his influence on the development of economics – and his 'steadfast adherence to the main tenets of classical liberalism' – have been sorely neglected.[10] He saw Cannan as a key figure in the transmission of the classical liberal tradition. As the teacher in the 1920s of Arnold Plant, Lionel Robbins, F. C. Benham, T. E. Gregory, W. H. Hutt and others, Cannan bequeathed a feeling of what Seldon called 'intellectual solidarity' and has a good claim to be regarded as the founder of the 'LSE School' of economic thought in the 1930s.

Throughout his life, Arthur Seldon was deeply influenced by

his experiences at the LSE. It was a time when classical economics had, in the eyes of many economists, been superseded by
'neoclassical' ideas. Economists were impressed by the notions of
market 'imperfections' and 'failures' and, both in macro and
micro policy issues, they saw a considerable role for the state to
put right what they saw as these failings.'Planning' was in vogue.
Government could help to stabilise the macroeconomy and it
could usefully intervene in particular sectors so as to ensure that
socially desirable outcomes were achieved.The source, in Britain,
of many of these ideas was the University of Cambridge, where
John Maynard (later Lord) Keynes and imperfect competition
theorists such as Joan Robinson were very influential.

The London School of Economics was founded by the
Fabian socialists Sidney and Beatrice Webb, Graham Wallas and
George Bernard Shaw in 1895, and by the 1930s it already had
the reputation of being a hotbed of socialism.The socialist theorists were mainly in the politics and history departments,
however, where outstanding socialists such as Harold Laski,
Eileen Power and H. L. Beales taught. The economics department at the LSE was not entirely free of such influences but it
was dominated by the leading classical liberal economists of the
day, notably Friedrich Hayek, Lionel (later Lord) Robbins and
Arnold (later Sir Arnold) Plant. By the time Seldon went to the
LSE, it had become one of the few remaining economics departments where classical economics was alive and well – and indeed
it was, in effect, launching a counter-attack on socialist economics. One of Seldon's contemporaries at the LSE, Stuart Waterhouse, who remained his friend for the rest of his life, has
described the 'exhilarating experience' of being at the School in
its 'golden days' (Chapter 2).

From a present-day vantage point, the most eminent of the
LSE economists in Seldon's day would appear to be Friedrich
Hayek and Ronald Coase, both of whom were subsequently
awarded Nobel Prizes in Economics.[11] Hayek was, of course,
one of the leading economists of the twentieth century, the
instigator of the revival of 'Austrian' economics, and originator

of the idea of competition as a 'process of discovery'. In the 1930s, when Seldon first came across him at the LSE, he was engaged in the revival of Austrian thought and mounting powerful critiques of socialist planning.[12] In Seldon's words, 'The Austrian school had almost fallen out of sight until Hayek introduced it into the LSE.'[13] He was also, from the 1930s onwards, the leading opponent of Keynes's ideas. Furthermore, Hayek played an important part in the founding of the Institute of Economic Affairs (see Chapter 4) and thereafter wrote a number of influential papers for the Institute. Seldon always felt and acknowledged the influence of Hayek and, during his time at the Institute, when he was frequently in contact with Hayek, Seldon was able through his editing to help him to spread his ideas to a wide audience and indeed to influence the governments of Margaret Thatcher. Hayek was eventually awarded the very high distinction of the Companion of Honour (CH) on the recommendation of Mrs Thatcher as Prime Minister.

Ronald Coase, who graduated from the LSE in 1931, was a young lecturer when Seldon was there. Coase had been a student of Arnold Plant and became a pioneer of the analysis of the economics of property rights and the legal framework of markets, eventually receiving the Nobel Prize in Economics in 1991 in recognition of his work and becoming one of the twentieth century's most prominent and most frequently cited economists because of his seminal contributions.[14] Coase is best known for two articles that discuss fundamental issues. 'The nature of the firm' (1937) explores why firms exist, and 'The problem of social cost', which led to the 'Coase Theorem' (so labelled by George Stigler, another Nobel Prizewinner in Economics), which suggests that the problem of externalities can be overcome by well-defined property rights. In both cases, Coase emphasised the importance of transactions costs (the costs incurred in making economic exchanges). Coase was one of the economists who helped to move economics back towards the classical concept of 'political economy', which was a trend much approved by Seldon, who became concerned that the increasing emphasis on

formal models and mathematical analysis was divorcing economists from contact with real problems.

As well as Hayek and Coase, two other outstanding economists at the LSE in Seldon's time were Lionel (later Lord)
Robbins and Arnold (later Sir Arnold) Plant. Lionel Robbins, at
the time regarded as the leader of the LSE economists. was an
economist with 'Austrian' views who was a prolific writer, both
on theory and on contemporary issues, and who produced critiques of planning and protectionism.[15] Robbins also published,
in 1932, one of the period's most significant works on the meth-
odology of economics, *An Essay on the Nature and Significance of
Economic Science*.[16] Robbins argued against the view that economics is concerned only with material welfare or with 'economic' motives. Rather, according to Robbins, it should be
correctly seen as 'the science which studies human behaviour as
a relationship between ends and scarce means which have alternative uses'. It was the presence of scarcity which was the key to
economic analysis, hence the need for economising. Economic
analysis was applicable to all aspects of human choice and behaviour, not merely those relating to material goods or production.
It could therefore be applied, for example, to the artistic and
cultural activities in which Robbins was particularly interested.
More generally, Robbins's view of economics opened the door
for economists to use their methods of analysis across a broad
range of activities – as indeed Seldon did, both in his writings
and in his editorial work. Robbins was another figure with
whom Seldon became reacquainted at the IEA. Robbins contributed to a number of its publications and Seldon described
him as '… next to Keynes, probably the most influential British
economist of his day'.[17]

Arnold Plant was another influential figure in Seldon's life.
He was impressed by the young Seldon and employed him as
research assistant after he graduated. Plant, like Robbins, was a
great believer in the power of market forces and the benefits of
competition. Moreover, he recognised that competitive markets
promote liberal values, overcoming forces of prejudice and

discrimination. Plant was, for example, concerned about the growing problem of race relations throughout the world. 'Western civilisation implies the breakdown of privilege and caste in the search for greater effectiveness of co-operation,'[18] he wrote. Plant was a very practical economist who served on the Monopolies and Restrictive Practices Commission, wrote about competition policy and, in a number of papers in the 1930s, analysed the effects of government intervention in the rail and road industries. He also launched some of the earliest explorations into the nature of property rights, the economic functions of ownership, and the relationship between the legal framework and the working of market forces,[19] stimulating the work that Ronald Coase carried forward. Plant, among all the LSE economists, was probably the closest to Seldon, and Plant helped him at various points in his career. Most crucially, Plant recommended Seldon to the newly forming Institute of Economic Affairs in 1956 when it was searching for an Editorial Director (see Chapter 4 below). Seldon's move to the IEA was, as explained in Chapter 4, the most important event in his working life.

The leading LSE economists, especially Hayek, Robbins and Plant, were therefore all considerable influences on Seldon's life and thought, and his career remained intertwined with theirs in his work at the IEA.

One other economist who influenced Seldon significantly was less well known and was not at the LSE, but came to his attention because of a reading list produced by Robbins for his students. Eugen von Böhm-Bawerk, an Austrian economist, wrote a paper entitled 'Macht oder Oconomisches Gesetz', which was published in 1914 but not translated into English until 1931, as 'Political power or economic law'.[20] Böhm-Bawerk argued that political power will eventually succumb to the superior power of the market. It was a point that greatly impressed Seldon, and he mentions it on several occasions in his writings as confirming his view that liberalism will eventually triumph. As Seldon put it in a paper written in 1978, 'politicians would have to defer to the people who are uniquely enfranchised by it [the market]'.[21] Later he argued that, recalling Böhm-Bawerk, in the 1990s people were finding ways of escaping from overweening governments and their actions were already beginning to curb the power of politicians.[22, 23]

The war years

Seldon graduated from the LSE in 1937 with first-class honours and was thereafter appointed research assistant to Arnold Plant (from 1937 to 1940). Just before war broke out, on Plant's advice, Arthur changed his name by deed poll from Slaberdain to Seldon.[24] For a brief period before he was called up for military service, Seldon was employed in conducting surveys during an episode in his career that might well have gone unnoticed had it not been for the recollections of Basil Yamey, later professor at the LSE and Seldon's friend, who worked with him at that time. A hitherto unpublished note from Yamey on that period is included in Chapter 2.

When his call-up came in 1941, Seldon was transferred to North Africa to assist in the logistical aspects of the invasion of Italy. He told Tame, however, that his broader political and intellectual interests found an outlet.

> He was concerned about the inefficiency of the Army's distribution of food and clothing, given that there were no prices to reflect relative scarcities, and he is said to have written to Arnold Plant along those lines. More generally, he realised that the Army's educational structure was, during the war, largely dominated by socialists of varying hue. Much of its published material and lecture programmes were propaganda for 'socialist justice', economic planning and a vision of the 'new order' to follow the war. The burdens of his military duties were not too onerous to prevent Seldon from trying to do something to counter this socialist bias. As

well as organising a number of lectures, on 20 December 1944 Seldon produced the first issue of *Valjean Times*, an eight-page weekly newspaper for his unit. The paper was a mixture of light news items, sports news, announcements, letters and articles. Brief but more serious features by Army contributors included such articles as 'War and the Evolution of Sex Equality', 'Democracy and Fascism in Italy', and 'The Tragedy of Poland'. Other articles dealt with post-war policy toward Germany, post-war colonial policy and Labour Party policy toward Greece. One writer, a Corporal V. Shewry, of the Seldon frame of mind, proposed the commercialism of the BBC and the introduction of competition in British radio broadcasting. However, unlike the Army Educational Bureau, Seldon attempted to maintain a modicum of political balance and objectivity. The regular 'The World About Us' feature balanced a socialist academic writer with Norman Tiptaft, the Liberal Lord Mayor of Birmingham in 1941–42 and a classical liberal who supported Sir Ernest Benn's Society of Individualists.[25] Given the pro-socialist mood of the time, an objective and rational temper was in itself a radical venture. The strongest sentiments were expressed by Seldon himself in one of his editorials on the postwar world. 'At Home', he hoped, 'we may look to conditions in which man can live his life according to his own conception of life. The philosophers call this "liberty", and there is no better good'. The prospects of Beveridge's plans for social security elicited the mild warning that 'to make social security possible we must retain the spirit of enterprise and independence without which it will degenerate into irresponsibility and sloth'.[26]

Seldon also described to Tame some of the problems he encountered during his war service.

Seldon's wartime service, whilst not in the front line, provided a number of close shaves. Whilst waiting to disembark from his troop ship in the Bay of Algiers, he was dive-bombed by Stukas – a fact made more disconcerting when he discovered that he was standing next to a major ammunition magazine. His troop ship was also hit by a torpedo in 1944 and he and his fellows were further strafed and bombed as they made their way to their barracks. During the later stages of the war Seldon accompanied his Brigade to Monte Cassino. Then, whilst in Italy, Seldon contracted a serious infection that severely affected his joints.[27] In 1945 he was returned by hospital ship to Britain, where he was hospitalised in Harrogate,[28] before being demobilised in the same year.

Early post-war years

On his demobilisation, Seldon used his war gratuity to purchase a small house, 'Brae Tor', in Crouch End, into which he, his brother Sid and Mrs Marks moved. According to Tame, he considered three possible career directions at this time: to return to academia, to seek a commercial career, or to enter politics professionally.

> The last of these options had already been offered to him before the end of the war. Seldon's friend Arthur Shenfield had been put in charge of the selection of Liberal Party candidates for the north of England and had asked him to become a Parliamentary candidate. At that moment, however, Seldon's hospitalisation put all thought of this political opening from his mind.
>   An academic career at this point would have put severe strains on Seldon's precarious financial position. Fortunately, something of a half-way-house option arose.

In January 1946 Seldon accepted the Editorship of *Store* magazine, a journal for larger department stores. The job enabled him to continue his academic interest in the economics of the retail industry whilst completing his MSc Econ started under Plant in 1938. It led to a close relation with Leonard Harris, owner and Managing Director of the renowned Browns of Chester and an active Liberal politician.

At about this time Plant, who knew that Marks and Spencer were seeking a scholar to research and write their company history, suggested Seldon to Simon Marks and Israel Sief who commissioned him to start a 'structural analysis' of the company. However, the Board of Directors, after examining Seldon's draft outline for the research, decided that the perceptiveness and rigour of Seldon's analysis would reveal too many commercially sensitive secrets of their trade. The project was cancelled, but Seldon was paid a not ungenerous sum of £100 for his initial work.

Meeting Marjorie

Becoming the editor of *Store* magazine had a particularly happy outcome for Seldon because it led to his meeting in 1946 with his future wife, Marjorie Perrott (née Willett), to whom he was married for 57 years. As described by Tame, based on his conversations with Seldon, the course of events was as follows:

> In March 1946, Marjorie, a 26 year old war-widow with a small adopted son, Michael (Perrott), had answered a *Times* advertisement for the post of assistant to the editor of the catalogue for ExhibitionDesign '46. Having had some writing experience and being a member of the National Union of Journalists (NUJ), she had been engaged by its editor, W. H. Newman, who was also the

owner of several magazines including *Store*, to work on a
catalogue of exhibits for an exhibition entitled 'Britain
Can Make It'. Amongst her tasks was ferrying papers
from the catalogue's office in the Board of Trade, off
Victoria Street, to the offices of *Store*, which were above
the Lilley and Skinner shoe shop in Oxford Street. Here
she met Arthur, who struck her first as an attractive man,
but perhaps somewhat intimidating. This impression was
reinforced by several heated telephone calls she had
overheard between Newman and Seldon. 'Arthur Seldon
is like a French cook, always giving notice!' Newman had
once exploded. In fact, Newman, aware that Seldon was
eager to enlarge his knowledge of the structure of British
retailing, had struck a somewhat hard bargain with the
young economist, and had acquired his services at a
lower than normal salary. This had further contributed to
Seldon's determination to maintain an independent line
in his editorial endeavours, a line not always amenable to
the views of the journal's owner.

The first meeting between Arthur and Marjorie took place
in the editor's office at *Store* magazine, when Marjorie heard
Arthur give Gamages (the retail store) a severe reprimand on the
telephone for their failure to deliver a sofa to his house in
Crouch End at the time promised. Marjorie realised that Arthur,
though generally of an even temperament, was capable of losing
his temper, particularly when faced with obvious inefficiency.
Despite the heated telephone calls, Marjorie was not put off and,
as Tame notes,

> Seldon could not have proved too intimidating and
> Marjorie – herself of an intellectual disposition – found
> herself increasingly drawn to the intelligent, idealistic and
> entertaining young man. Their first meeting was followed
> rapidly by many others. They would dine at the National
> Liberal Club (of which Arthur was a member before

moving to the Reform in 1950), taking drives in
Marjorie's Singer 9 car in the country around her
parents' Kentish home. Arthur was soon to meet her
parents, and Marjorie also met Arthur's brother Sid – but
not, at that time, his mother.

During 1947 love between Arthur and Marjorie was
kindled and flourished and they decided that they wished
to marry. But there were difficulties. One was financial.
Arthur was already supporting his mother and paying the
mortgage on the home in Crouch End. It was not
financially feasible for Arthur to support a second home
and household. Marjorie was a member of the Willett
family, owners of a building firm started in Brighton in
the 1880s which by 1914 had created a fortune. However,
her grandfather, Thomas Willett, was a younger son and
the business had gone to the elder son William (the
progenitor of 'Daylight Saving'). Marjorie's father,
Wilfred, was poor. He had been a medical student who
left his studies at Cambridge to serve in the armed forces
but his prospective medical career was cut short when he
sustained a terrible wound in the Great War.[29]

Perhaps even more serious an obstacle, however,
related to Arthur's family. Mrs Marks had made many
sacrifices for her adopted son but was very much a
woman of her time and class, and the horizons and
attitudes that accompanied them. She had always
envisaged Arthur marrying a girl of her own faith, who
would join her in the family home. Indeed, she thought
she had already found a suitable match – a relative of her
deceased second husband. The challenge of the
Holocaust to the very existence of Jewish people also,
understandably, made thoughts of 'marrying out' seem
even less acceptable. Arthur's sense of duty and gratitude
to his mother was enormous and admirable. He even
feared that, frail as she then was, the shock of an
unapproved marriage might make her seriously ill.

During 1947 one obstacle – the financial one – was removed. Marjorie's grandmother died and left her a small trust which could be realised into capital – enough to pay a deposit and furnish a house. In this year both Marjorie and Arthur had become actively involved in Liberal Party campaigns. Marjorie's father – a former Christian, who felt that the Church was insufficiently militant in the cause of the poor – was a convinced Communist, but one who had been drawn to that position from genuine benevolence. It was this genuine benevolence and idealism that enabled him to recognise the same sensibility in the young Seldon. The two men never argued about politics and remained mutually fond and respectful to the end of Willett's life in 1961. Marjorie herself had shared her father's ideals, and had, during a brief residence in South Africa before the start of the war, written articles for its newspaper there.[30] However, even before meeting Arthur she had begun to have doubts about the viability and results of communism. Exposure to discussions of classical liberalism – and a morally motivated and intellectually rigorous alternative to communism – thus found fertile intellectual ground. She recalls attending a lecture[31] by one of the stalwarts of liberalism, Isaac Foot (father of Michael, who was later to become leader of the Labour Party) and was soon drawn into Arthur's Liberal Party activism.

A possible resolution of Arthur's problem with his mother might have emerged in that same year, when Arthur, at his brother Sid's suggestion, invited her and Sid to join him and Marjorie – who was introduced as 'a Liberal Party worker' to his mother – at a performance of *Rigoletto* at Covent Garden. Mrs Marks, who had perhaps been picking up the emotional vibrations rather than the musical ones, asked Sid during an interval 'Who is that girl?'. Her suspicions were not allayed and an uncomfortable scene ensued. Although Marjorie did spend the night at Crouch End, at Sid's insistence, the frosty relationship that had been established prevented her from seeing Mrs Marks for another three years.

In 1948 Arthur and Marjorie decided to marry – but in secret – in the hope that eventually his mother might be reconciled to a *fait accompli*. The marriage took place on 23 February 1948, at Tonbridge Registry Office. Arthur was accompanied by his friend Basil Yamey, a South African post-graduate LSE student before the war. Yamey – who became a greatly respected economist in his own right – had recently returned from South Africa to a lectureship under Plant at the LSE. His intercession at the ceremony was invaluable when Arthur failed to respond correctly to the Registrar's question 'Occupation of father?' 'He died when I was two' was not acceptable, and Basil interjected with 'Merchant' – a white lie enshrined on the marriage certificate.

The Seldons had a short honeymoon in Eastbourne, and then lived for a few months with Marjorie's parents at their home, The Rosery, in Matfield. They used Marjorie's car to drive to Tunbridge Wells station from where they commuted to Charing Cross, an easy distance for Marjorie from Fleet Street, where she was working in a public relations firm. Weekends were spent searching for a house, and eventually they found a suitable property in Petts Wood, near Orpington in Kent, to which they moved in 1948. Arthur continued to support his mother until she died in her eighties.

2

The LSE and the early war years: some reflections by contemporaries

The influence of the LSE

As already explained, and as is clear from Seldon's writings,[1] his time at the LSE was a period when the classical liberal ideas that were already forming in his mind were stimulated and developed by his contacts with Robbins, Hayek, Plant and his other teachers. Furthermore, like most students, he learned at least as much from discussion and argument with his fellow students as from his teachers.

Seldon was always appreciative of what the LSE economists had done for him and he maintained his association with the LSE throughout his life: he was a tutor and staff examiner there from 1946 to 1966 (until his IEA work prevented him from continuing), and in 2001 he had the distinction of becoming a Fellow of the LSE. In Seldon's view, the LSE of the 1930s lived on in the IEA from the late 1950s onwards.[2] His IEA post gave him the opportunity to develop the classical liberal ideas he had found so attractive during his student days, to work out their practical implications for the post-war British economy and

society and, in combination with like-minded scholars, to publicise the results. For him, the founding of the IEA and his
appointment as Editorial Director represented 'the fulfilment of
my postgraduate hopes of 1938–39'.[3]

He remained friends throughout his life with two of his contemporaries at the LSE – Stuart Waterhouse, a fellow under-
graduate (two years behind Seldon), and Basil Yamey (later a
distinguished professor at the School), who was a postgraduate
student there in the late 1930s. Their recollections provide some
details of Seldon's activities just before he began his wartime
service in the British army. Previously unpublished papers by
Waterhouse and Yamey appear below. The first, by Waterhouse,
records his recollections of Seldon at the LSE during the School's
'golden years' when they, and some contemporaries who later
became famous, were fortunate to be taught by some of the
leading economists of the time. The second, by Yamey, concerns
his friendship with Seldon in the 1940s, including the time
when they were together in the Wartime Social Survey, where
Seldon worked as the random sampler, in the early part of the
1939–45 war.

Arthur Seldon at the LSE
Stuart Waterhouse

> Arthur and I first met at the London School of
> Economics in October 1936. We became friends and our
> friendship lasted for 69 years until his death in October
> 2005. Not that it was friendship at first sight. We were
> not exactly well matched. I was a rather naïve youth of
> 18 from North Wales. He was a more mature cockney,
> who was the following year to gain a first class honours
> degree in Economics, a subject of which I was totally
> ignorant.
>
> We met in the Liberal Society. I was a Liberal born
> and bred. Arthur was a Liberal by conviction and

conversion – he had dabbled with communism in his youth. We used to meet most afternoons for tea in the college refectory and put the world to rights. Arthur was fond of recalling that our Liberal Society comprised ourselves and 12 Egyptian students. This was an exaggeration. I cannot remember more than six – probably asylum seekers from King Farouk.

Arthur, who, when I first knew him, was called Arthur Slaberdain (he changed his name in 1939 at Professor Plant's suggestion), was not in those days a forceful character and was plagued by a bad stammer. I was more attracted to the chairman of the Society, John Daniel Dale-Green, a colourful personality who had boxed for the University and appointed himself manager of my political career with the result that I was elected to the Student Union executive in my first year.

Arthur, meanwhile, quietly pursued his objective of converting us to classical liberal economics, untainted by the prevailing Keynesian doctrine of the time. One incident I recall involved us earning a reproof from our great friend, Seaborne Davies (reader in law). We had jointly written a letter to *The Times* regarding the reorganisation of the railways, a subject on which we were, of course, experts. Our crime was to use the LSE address and Seaborne wagged his finger at us in no uncertain manner.

The Liberal Society was, however, peripheral to what Arthur and I were really doing at the School in what we were agreed was its Golden Age. I do not make that claim lightly. An educational institution which could boast a staff that included the economists Lionel Robbins, Arnold Plant, Friedrich Hayek, the economic historians Richard Tawney and Eileen Power and the political scientist, Harold Laski, supported by such young lions as Ronald Coase, Ronald Fowler, Frank Paish, Nicholas Kaldor and Ronald Edwards, would be remarkable by any standards. Most of them taught us both and we drank deep at their wells of learning and wisdom.

LSE was founded by Sidney and Beatrice Webb and Bernard Shaw in 1895. As co-founders also of the Fabian Society (in 1883) they no doubt hoped that the School would be a power-house for the socialist world they envisaged. The Webbs famously went to Soviet Russia in the 1930s and returned with the conclusive statement that they had 'seen the future'. We all make mistakes. Lloyd George at about the same time was impressed by Hitler.

Whatever the founding fathers had envisaged, LSE reached its full maturity in the 1930s under the able direction of Sir William Beveridge, previously a distinguished civil servant who had established the first labour exchanges. However, although according to St Mark's Gospel 'If a house be divided against itself that house cannot stand', that was not true of the LSE in the 1930s. It was indeed a house divided and flourished in spite of its division. On one hand we had committed socialists such as Richard Tawney, Eileen Power, Hugh Dalton (public finance economist) and Harold Laski and on the other hand the economists led by Lionel Robbins, Arnold Plant and Friedrich Hayek who belonged to the classic liberal school. In our no doubt prejudiced view it was the liberals who prevailed and gave the School its distinctive ethos and reputation.

To be a student in such an environment was an exhilarating experience. I came to the LSE in October 1936 and found myself plunged into a cosmopolitan student body of some 3,000 including 700 from overseas (mostly Indian and Chinese), attracted perhaps as much by the School's socialist reputation as by its academic eminence.

When it was the Liberal Society's turn to invite a speaker to address the Student Union we conceived the bold notion to bring over from his exile in Paris Alexander Kerensky, the last democratic leader of Russia before the Soviet Revolution of 1917. As Chairman of the Society (I had succeeded Dale-Green in 1937) it fell to me to introduce this historic figure to a packed and not too sympathetic house. Kerensky spoke in fast, unintelligible French, which his son manfully attempted (and failed) to interpret for our benefit. As far as I could understand, Kerensky was justifying his presidency of the Duma (the Russian parliament). It was very much a case of 'après moi, le deluge'.

I have to admit that the LSE's reputation as a hotbed of socialist thinking has survived all our attempts to paint a truer picture. Yet, when I consider the names of some of my distinguished contemporaries I can only smile in disbelief. The list includes Douglas Allen (Lord Croham and Head of the Civil Service during Harold Wilson's premiership), Sir Douglas Henley (Auditor General), Sir Huw Wheldon (Managing Director of the BBC), Harry Henry (Managing Director of the Thompson organisation and visiting Professor of Marketing, Bradford University), John Mitchell (Professor of Law), John Griffiths (Professor of Law) and of course Arthur Seldon who has been described as a 'towering figure in the development of political and economic thought and practice from the 1960s onwards' and 'one of the principal classical liberal figures in the last hundred years'. In fairness to my socialist friends, I must add the names of Arthur Lewis (economist, Nobel Prizewinner in 1979 and first principal of the University of the West Indies) and Michael (Lord) Young, who wrote the Labour Party manifesto for the 1945 General Election and went on to found the Consumers' Association (publishers of *Which*), the Advisory Centre for Education and the Open University. Michael, whom I succeeded as secretary of the LSE Student Union, was described by Noel Annan in his book *Our Age* as 'the most original and influential sociologist of his time'.

When I graduated in June 1939, the war clouds were already gathering and soon Arthur and I found ourselves in a very different environment from the LSE: privates in the Army, but separated by great distances. We had enjoyed the best of times at the School and our memories of those great days would last a lifetime, as did our friendship.

Arthur Seldon in the early years of the war
Basil Yamey

Arthur and I first met early in 1939, at the London School of Economics. He was then research assistant to Professor (later Sir) Arnold Plant. The main research project was a study of the operating costs of a large number of department stores which annually provided details of their costs on a consistent basis. Under Plant's supervision, Arthur collated the data and analysed them in various ways. The participating companies were given the summarised, sub-divided and analysed cost statistics, so that each could compare its own cost performance with the average for all department stores in the sample and relevant sub-samples. The annual statistical findings formed the basis of an article by Plant in *Economica*.

Arthur also assisted Plant in other ways. In turn, Arthur attended Plant's lectures and seminars as well as those of others, for example those given by Lionel Robbins and Hayek at the LSE. Arnold Plant had a considerable influence on Arthur, both academically and personally, as Arthur was to acknowledge publicly on many occasions. Plant had the gift of unobtrusively encouraging young colleagues and students in whom he saw promise.

I came to the LSE, from South Africa, in December 1938. I was to work towards an M.Sc in economics and had the good fortune of having Plant and Ronald (later Sir Ronald) Edwards as my joint supervisors. Through Plant, I must have met Arthur. But we did not really get to know each other at all well before 1940.

Early in 1940, I decided to discontinue my graduate studies and to return to South Africa to enlist in the armed forces there. I informed Plant accordingly. He thought what I proposed was a good idea. But he had a better suggestion. He had been asked by Mr Duff Cooper, Minister for Information, to organise a unit which would conduct surveys of public opinion and report the findings to the government. The Ministry was particularly interested in the state of the public's morale and in the man-in-the-street's expectations, views and worries concerning the war and its conduct. Plant asked me to join the unit as a temporary civil servant and to take responsibility for running the show on a day-to-day basis under his supervision. At the time, he held a prominent and influential position in the Ministry of Supply. I would report to him at regular intervals and consult him as necessary.

Plant acquired a large office for the Wartime Social Survey – in premises belonging to the Royal Institute of International Affairs ('Chatham House'). I was installed there, with two charming young secretaries. Soon teams of investigators were recruited and the first questionnaires compiled, the latter with the valuable assistance of LSE people who drifted in and out of the office – including two future Nobel Laureates in Economics, Arthur Lewis and Ronald Coase, both of whom were to recognise their intellectual indebtedness to Plant.

At this point, Arthur entered the scene, much to my pleasure. His task, assigned to him by Plant, was to be our random sampler. He had to compile a suitable-sized random sample of people on the electoral roll for each city or town where public opinion was to be polled. Arthur set about this task as conscientiously, systematically and accurately as was to be expected. He also worked with me on analysing the completed questionnaires – filled in by our investigators who visited the selected respondents. He also reviewed the reports I drafted, and generally did far more for the Wartime Social Survey than he was required to do. I believe he also continued to do some work as Plant's research assistant. Arthur was a great help and we got to know each other very well in the few months before he received his call-up papers.

The office was a happy place with Arthur around. In spite of the grim news of the war, the atmosphere was enjoyable. We often went to one or other Soho restaurant for lunch – Soho prices being very reasonable in those days – usually accompanied by our two secretaries. Conversation ranged from questions of political economy to more mundane and local matters.

It was intended that the Wartime Social Survey would operate as a separate unit without any known connection with government. But this was not to be. In those suspicious days, the press, especially newspapers in areas being surveyed, soon began to report on the activities of our teams of investigators who were asking questions such as 'What do you think Hitler will do next?' or 'When do you think the war will be over?' In one or two places, investigators were actually taken into police custody, on complaints from members of the public that they were trouble-makers, subversives or even spies. It was necessary then to disclose that the Wartime Social Survey was a respectable outfit which belonged to the 'Min of Inf' – and our investigators were dubbed 'Cooper's Snoopers'.

Nevertheless, the work continued, even after the

bombing of London and other places had started. But
operations became progressively more difficult. Moreover,
the succession of surveys had established conclusively
that civilian morale was high and that the overwhelming
majority of the public was seriously over-optimistic. We
joked that we were responsible for Churchill's 'blood,
sweat and tears' and similar statements. The unit was
brought to an end in November 1940.

Arthur and I met again after the war. I returned to
London in 1948. We resumed our friendship which had
been maintained by correspondence in the meantime.
Arthur continued his LSE connection after the war. For
many years, he served as a diligent and scrupulous
external examiner. He was also a Senior Tutor for the
Commerce Degree Bureau which helped to prepare
external students for the University of London degree,
the Bachelor of Commerce (B.Com). The Bureau was
another of Arnold Plant's initiatives, and was highly
valued by external students who chose to follow its
courses. Arthur took his duties very seriously. He read the
students' essays with great care; and I know that the
comments and suggestions he wrote on many of them
showed that cogency, encouragement and felicity of
language that he was to demonstrate so amply and
consistently in his work as Editorial Director at the
Institute of Economic Affairs. As the author of the first
Hobart Paper, I was an early beneficiary of Arthur's talent
as friendly critic and editor.

3

The effects of Arthur Seldon's upbringing

Arthur Seldon told Chris Tame that he saw little positive significance in his own Jewish background. He was, he explained to Tame, neither a religious believer in, nor a marked 'rebel' against, Judaism, and was not particularly interested in specific Jewish traditions merely as a social or traditional observance. According to Tame, Seldon

> jokingly asserted that he 'just happened', like Athena springing from the brow of Zeus, in his late teens. As a man of ideas, his real life – a life of the mind – really only comes into conscious focus at that time – and he himself sees little connection (with the exception of the lessons of working class self-help) between his background and his subsequent intellectual development.

It is, however, worth reflecting further on the 'Jewish dimension', which may well have been a significant factor in forming Seldon's views on economic and social issues, and particularly on government action, including state provision of 'welfare'.

Competition in a moral regime

The Chief Rabbi, Jonathan Sacks, has stressed the extent to which an inherent feature of Jewish traditions is competition within a regime of business honesty:

> ... the rabbis favoured markets and competition because they generated wealth, lowered prices, increased choice, reduced absolute levels of poverty, and in the course of time extended humanity's control over the environment, narrowing the extent to which we are the passive victims of circumstance and fate. Competition releases energy and creativity and serves the general good ... alongside the respect for markets went a sharp insistence on the ethics of business ... Canons of fair trading had to be established and policed, and much of Jewish law is taken up with these concerns.[1]

In the community into which Arthur Seldon was born and where he spent his life up to the age of fifteen (when Eva Marks remarried), poor as most people were, this ethical version of capitalism appears to have been realised. Competition was fierce in the markets in which the immigrants sold their labour services and in the markets for the products they produced. The successful could and did move rapidly up the economic and social scales. There was, however, cooperation as well as competition in the form of a well-established voluntary 'welfare' regime, in which the better off helped those who were temporarily in trouble to help themselves, and also gave aid to those more permanently disadvantaged. It was welfare without the state.

From the 1880s onwards, the East End of London was full of Jewish immigrants, mainly from Russia and Poland. In Russia, in particular, the Jews suffered persecution from which many chose to escape to England. Both Seldon's natural parents, Masha and Pinchas Margolis, who emigrated from Russia, and the émigré couple who adopted him, Eva and Marks Slaberdain, belonged

Arthur with his adoptive parents, Eva and Marks Slaberdain

Right: Arthur outside his adoptive father's boot sale and repair shop in the East End of London

Below: Arthur (circled) with Class 6 at the Dempsey Street Elementary School

Above: Arthur (seated at left) with his older brothers (left to right) Cecil, Jack and Sidney, and sister Bessie, around 1926/7

Right: Arthur on graduation with first class honours from the London School of Economics in the summer of 1937

Above: Arthur on wartime military service in Algiers, 1943/4
Below: Warrant Officer Seldon, 1943

Left: Arthur and Marjorie on their wedding day, 23 February 1948, outside Tonbridge Registry Office

Below: The wedding party: (from left) Marjorie's godmother, Muriel Stagg; the best man, Basil Yamey (later a professor of economics and an IEA author); Arthur; Marjorie's adopted son, Michael; Marjorie; Marjorie's mother, Eileen Willett; and Michael's governess, Miss Benton ('Benny')

Family group on the occasion of Arthur's nephew Ramsey
Margolis's Bah Mitzvah in November 1964. Pictured from left are:
Jack Levinson (husband of Arthur's sister Bess), Bess Levinson,
Haime Valins (husband of Arthur's cousin Maise), Martin Valins,
Maise Valins, Arthur, Bess's daughter Marilyn, Anne Margolis (wife of
Arthur's older brother Jack), Marjorie Seldon, Ramsey (formerly
Alan) Margolis (son of Jack), Jack Margolis, Sidney Margolis, Rosie
Copen (the wife of Arthur's Uncle Ben, the brother of his natural
mother Masha), Uncle Ben, Pearl Margolis (wife of Arthur's brother
Cecil) and Cecil Margolis

Arthur and Marjorie's three sons: (left to right) Michael, Peter and
Anthony

Mont Pelerin Society group in the early 1980s. Front row, from left: Antonio Martino (Italian Finance Minister), Herbert Giersch, Manual Ayau, Nobel Laureate James Buchanan, Nobel Laureate Milton Friedman, Chiaki Nishiyama. Second row, from left: Max Hartwell, Henry Manne, Gary Becker, Richard Ware, Arvid Fredburg, Ralph Harris. Third row, from left: Edwin Feulner, Allen Wallis, Carl-Johan Westholm, Rose Friedman, Peter Bernholz, Charles King, Arthur Seldon, Leonard Liggio.

Arthur (at left) and Ralph Harris at the Institute of Economic
Affairs in Eaton Place

to this community of recent immigrants where voluntary action, to help oneself and to help one's fellow community members, was the norm.

Beatrice Webb on the East End Jews

To appreciate what the Jewish East End was like in the late nineteenth and early twentieth centuries, a particularly useful source is a vivid description of the East End Jews in the last years of the nineteenth century, not long before Masha and Pinchas Margolis arrived, in an essay written by Beatrice Potter, who became Beatrice Webb when she married Sidney Webb. The Webbs were, of course, leading Fabian socialists, co-founders of the LSE in 1895 (Chapter 2 above) and of the *New Statesman* in 1913. At the time Beatrice wrote the essay, she was about thirty. It was a few years before she married Sidney Webb, at a time when she was one of the researchers on the monumental social survey carried out by her cousin, Charles Booth, at the end of the nineteenth century, entitled *Life and Labour of the People of London*. Volume 1 of Booth's survey, published in 1889,[2] contains several essays on 'Special subjects', one of which is Beatrice Potter's on 'The Jewish community'. She describes the 'distinct economic and social life' of the 'Jewish settlement' in 'the midst of the chaotic elements of East London'.[3] The community in which Arthur Seldon grew up must have been similar to the one Beatrice Webb (to use her more familiar name) describes.

After tracing the history of Jewish settlement in London, which began in the late seventeenth century, Webb explains that the East End Jews stood outside the institutions that had been established to serve the needs of the main body of Jews in England, partly because of their 'extreme poverty' and partly because of the 'foreign habits and customs of the vast majority of East End Jews'.[4] Most were 'either foreigners or children of foreigners' and the dominant nationalities were Russian and Polish. They rarely attended the larger synagogues. The religious-minded had formed associations, called Chevras, which, in Webb's words, 'combine the functions of a benefit club for death, sickness, and the solemn rites of mourning with that of public worship and the study of the Talmud'.[5] There were thirty or forty such Chevras,[6] each of which was usually named after the district from which the majority of its members had emigrated.

These Chevras, according to Webb, supplied the 'social and religious needs of some 12,000 to 15,000 foreign Jews'. Commenting on a proposal to replace the Chevras with a large synagogue, 'endowed by the charity of the West', which she thought unwise, Webb explained the benefits of voluntary action within communities, observing,

> it is easy to overlook the influence for good of self-creating, self-supporting, and self-governing communities; small enough to generate public opinion and the practical supervision of private morals, and large enough to stimulate charity, worship and study by communion and example.[7]

Outside the larger synagogues and the Chevras, according to Webb, there were another 20,000 to 30,000 other Jews 'too poor or too indifferent to attend regularly a place of worship' who nevertheless 'cling with an almost superstitious tenacity to the habits and customs of their race'.[8] There was considerable social and economic mobility but, as individuals rise out of this poor group, their places are, she said, taken by new immigrants from Poland or Russia and it forms 'a permanent layer of poverty verging on destitution'. This group was not, however, outside the Jewish charitable regime. It was connected to the Jewish middle and upper classes by a 'downward stream of charity and personal service, a benevolence at once so widespread and so thorough-going, that it fully justifies the saying "All Israel are brethren"'.[9]

Of the 'many educational and charitable institutions connected with the East End Jewish life', says Webb, one of the most significant is the Jewish Board of Guardians, founded in 1868.

The Board of Guardians, however, Webb pointed out, gave little in the way of outdoor relief. It helped people to help themselves. Much of the aid it gave was in the form of loans for trade and business purposes and business capital which allowed the recipients 'to raise themselves permanently from the ranks of those who depend on charity for subsistence'.[10] There were very few paupers in the East End Jewish community. Webb seemed unsure whether to applaud the regime she found because it encouraged self-help, or to criticise it because it encouraged self-employment and intensified competition among the 'small masters'. Her distaste for competition emerges.

> If we help a man to exist without work, we demoralize
> the individual and encourage the growth of a parasitic or
> pauper class. If, on the other hand, we raise the recipient
> permanently from the condition of penury ... we save
> him at the cost of all those who compete with him.[11]

Because of the circumstances faced by the Russian and Polish Jews, they were bound together by 'common suffering and mutual helpfulness' but isolated from surrounding communities. Webb observed that although the typical Russian or Polish Jew arrived with 'no ready-made skill of a marketable character', he tended to rise quickly to the 'higher provinces of production'. Even the poorest Jew, says Webb, has inherited through his religion a trained intellect; and another reason for the economic and social mobility of the Jewish population is the absence of a rigid class system. The East End Jews, often resented by their Gentile neighbours, are 'a race of brain-workers competing with a class of manual labourers'.[12] To the East End Jew, manual work is just the first rung on the employment ladder.

Webb saw the East End Jews as law abiding, impressed by the sanctity of contract and keen to compete.

> ... it is by competition, and by competition alone, that
> the Jew seeks success ... the foreign Jew totally ignores

all social obligations other than keeping the law of the land, the maintenance of his own family, and the charitable relief of co-religionists.[13]

She ends her chapter by comparing the East End Jew to Ricardo's picture of economic man:

> … an Always Enlightened Selfishness, seeking employment or profit with an absolute mobility of body and mind, without pride, without preference, without interests outside the struggle for the existence and the welfare of the individual and the family.[14]

Webb added that 'the prophetic deduction of the Hebrew economist' would be fulfilled in the East End – the majority of manual workers would earn a bare subsistence wage. Nevertheless, she seemed to find, in the Jewish East End, a community that in many respects she admired even though, as a budding social engineer, she could not entirely approve, and she was apparently surprised that in a community where competition prevailed (in the markets for both products and labour) there was evidence of so much cooperation and the voluntary provision of 'welfare'. Instead of some outside body helping the members of the community, they themselves made provision for their less fortunate members or those who needed a temporary helping hand.

Victorian virtues

Gertrude Himmelfarb, commenting on Webb's ambivalence towards the East End Jews, argues with some force that Beatrice Webb was 'a Victorian more than a socialist'. Consequently, according to Himmelfarb, Webb responded well to the 'Victorian virtues' she perceived in Jewish East End life, such as hard work, thrift, sobriety, respect for the law, self-reliance and devotion to family and community, even though such a community is quite different from the controlled and regulated society that Fabian socialists would favour.[15]

Instead of values having to be imposed, so that 'social values' prevailed over the pursuit of self-interest,

> In the Jewish community, she found a very different kind of society, one that was eminently moral but where moral values reposed in the individual, where individuals were encouraged to be responsible, self-reliant, and self-disciplined, and where those values were expressed in their relations to their family, their community, their religion, and, not least, their work.[16]

As Himmelfarb says, 'It's curious to find a socialist praising a Jewish ethic which was also, as she recognized, a capitalist ethic.'[17] The kind of society that Beatrice Webb discovered in East London – which evidently caused her a degree of intellectual unease – was the one in which Arthur Seldon's natural parents, and later the family that adopted him, lived. It would not have changed much by the time he was born in 1916. It is hardly surprising, therefore, that, as he grew up, and given his family circumstances, he should have been impressed by the benefits of the 'Victorian virtues' of self-help, hard work, respect for the law and devotion to family and community, and that in his writings in later life he should have emphasised the advantages of such virtues as compared with state control and regulation. He harks back, in his written work, to the community in which he grew up and how people in such communities had been able to escape from poverty because they lived in a capitalist system.[18] In the Jewish community in the East End, Seldon saw for himself how competition and cooperation can go hand in hand and how effective voluntary welfare provision can be. That experience may well ever after have coloured his views about government action in general, and in particular action to establish and maintain a 'welfare state.'

PART II

THE INSTITUTE OF ECONOMIC AFFAIRS

4

Seldon's move to the IEA: a turning point in life

Early post-war career

In the previous three chapters, we can begin to see the influence exerted on Arthur Seldon by his background and to discern the source of his ideas about the economy and society.

To summarise, a boy, following the death of his natural parents when he was only two, is brought up in a Jewish family which was poor if not in abject poverty. He lives in a community where hard work, self-help and caring for other members of the community are the norms, and he observes the benefits of self-help when his adoptive father dies but turns out to have made reasonable provision for his mother. His mother too believes in helping herself and in providing for her family by working. She finds work, despite the difficult economic circumstances of the time, and also receives some benefits from the Jewish welfare system. The boy, left out of the grammar school that he has decided he should attend to further his education, collaborates with another boy in similar circumstances and, by his perseverance, obtains entry to the school. He receives a good education in the course of which his imagination is fired by his history teacher, who discusses the elements of economic liberalism. He begins to move away from his early socialism towards liberal ideas. The boy's mother, despite being uneducated herself, insists that he should continue his education at university rather than, as she is urged, pressing him to go to work to supplement the family's earnings. Hence, the boy arrives at the London School of Economics in the mid-1930s, just at the time when several outstanding classical liberal economists (as well as numerous well-known socialists) are teaching there. The boy is inspired by classical liberal ideas and goes on to a first-class honours degree, followed by a research assistantship to one of his mentors, Professor Arnold Plant. That, in a nutshell, is the story of Arthur Seldon's first 21 years. Given the orientation of the LSE when he was a student, he could have become a leading socialist thinker. Instead – perhaps because he had observed and absorbed the benefits of voluntary action and self-help, and because of his Jewish background, as well as because of the influence of the LSE economists – he became a champion of market liberalism.

His career was interrupted, as were the careers of many of his contemporaries, by service in the British army during World War II, when he had little opportunity to pursue his interests in classical liberalism, though, as Tame points out, he took what opportunities he could. After the war, Seldon had to find work that would suit his talents. He was then faced with a choice between a return to academia, a career in politics or a position in commerce. His initial choice was commerce: as Chapter 1 explains, from 1946 to 1949 he worked for *Store* magazine, a publication for large department stores, where he gained experience of the retail trade. He then moved to work for a longer period of about eight years in the brewing industry, where he was employed as economic adviser to the Brewers' Society, the policy-forming central council of the industry, located in Dean's Yard, Westminster, and headed by Marshal of the Royal Air Force Lord Tedder, who had achieved fame as deputy to Eisenhower in the invasion of Europe. At that time, the brewers operated a 'tied house' system under which brewers owned public houses that stocked only their owners' products. Seldon had serious doubts about such a restrictive practice: Marjorie Seldon recalls that Arthur told her that Tedder himself was sceptical about the benefits of the system to the brewers. Seldon wrote several articles which argued that the brewers should loosen the link between their beer-producing role and their role as property owners of licensed premises. Not surprisingly, as he pointed out many years later in *Capitalism*, these articles 'raised eyebrows'[1] among the brewers.

The move to the IEA

While he was working at the Brewers' Society, he was approached in 1956 by the Liberal Lord Grantchester, who had been given his name by Arnold Plant, who enquired whether he would join the newly formed Institute of Economic Affairs. The founding of the Institute owed much to advice given by Friedrich Hayek to Antony (later Sir Antony) Fisher, its founder. In 1945, Fisher, who was disillusioned with the state of post-war Britain and was considering going into politics, went to Hayek for advice after he had read a *Readers' Digest* condensed version of Hayek's classic *The Road to Serfdom*. According to Fisher, Hayek's advice was to keep out of politics and to make an intellectual case by helping to form a 'scholarly research organisation to supply intellectuals in universities, schools, journalism and broadcasting with authoritative studies of the economic theory of markets and its application to practical affairs'.[2] Hayek was, in effect, giving Fisher the same message as he set out in *The Intellectuals and Socialism*[3] – that the intellectuals ('second hand dealers in ideas') have to be converted away from socialism. Once the general climate of opinion begins to change, the politicians will then follow.

Fisher went on to be a successful entrepreneur, founding Buxted Chickens, which opened up a mass market for chickens in Britain, reducing prices sufficiently to make chicken – previously regarded as a luxury item – an affordable dish for most people. His success as a businessman gave him the opportunity to act on Hayek's advice and so, with some colleagues, he started the IEA in 1955.[4] Ralph Harris was recruited as General Director from January 1957, and in the same year Arthur Seldon became part-time Editorial Adviser, working on several projects until he could join full time. As explained below, the advice given by Hayek was followed religiously by Fisher, Harris and Seldon: they avoided lobbying and close political encounters of all kinds, concentrating instead on making a clear and well-reasoned case in the Institute's publications. Fisher, who had a strong belief in the benefits of free markets, recognised the qualities of Harris and Seldon and was content to let them run the Institute with very little interference from him: he chaired the IEA trustees and was active in raising funds, but otherwise he gave them a free hand. Subsequently, Fisher had many ups and downs as a businessman but, when he died in 1988, he left a remarkable legacy in terms of the large number of think tanks, modelled generally on the IEA, which he helped to create all round the world.[5]

Arthur Seldon would have seemed a good choice for the fledgling IEA. By this time, he was 40 years old and had substantial working experience (ten years) in commerce. Moreover, he had credentials both as a classical liberal economist (having indeed been taught by Hayek, Robbins and Plant, among others at the LSE – see Chapter 1 above) and as an author, having written about market liberalism and about pensions (the latter being a topic to which he returned frequently in later years). His first published paper, which appeared in March 1937 when he was twenty and had just graduated ('The State versus the Market'[6]), is a review of a book by W. H. Hutt in which Seldon compares and contrasts socialism and capitalism, and explains the benefits of competition. He had also become active in Liberal Party circles.[7] In 1937, the party established a committee of inquiry into the distribution of property, chaired by Elliott Dodds. Seldon was asked by Dodds to draft the committee's report, *Ownership for All*, which argued against statist solutions to the perceived problem of the maldistribution of property: it was adopted by the party conference in 1938.[8] In 1941, the Liberal Party published a pamphlet by Seldon, *The Drift to the Corporate State*, which attacked corporatist forms of industrial organisation.[9] In all these papers can be seen early versions of the arguments in favour of competitive markets and against state monopoly which Seldon deployed to such effect in his later work. Another Liberal Party activity was a committee on the aged which Seldon chaired and whose report was endorsed by the Liberal Assembly in 1948.[10] His work on the committee brought him into contact with Sir William Beveridge, who had, in 1942, written a report on the social services that was very influential in the formation of the state pension system in Britain after World War II.[11] Seldon's first major project at the IEA was to write a paper on pensions (*Pensions in a Free Society*[12]), which was published in 1957.

A turning point in life

Once Seldon was established in the IEA, moving from part-time Editorial Adviser in 1957 to full-time Editorial Director in 1959, it soon became clear that he had found his rightful place, where he could pursue his interest in classical liberal ideas. From then on his work, as an author and as an editor, flourished. The early months at the IEA were, according to reports, rather chaotic. Seldon's secretary at the Brewers' Society, Heather Grange (later Owen), who moved with him to the IEA, recalls the problems of these early months at the Institute in Hobart Place as new equipment had to be set up '... in the midst of intense academic work and deadlines to be met'.[13] Nevertheless, she remembers, Seldon was already trying to push forward the work of the Institute, despite the administrative chaos. He was very active and visitors were '... swept up by AS's boundless enthusiasm'.

The move to the IEA was a genuine turning point in Seldon's life, providing him with a post that suited his talents particularly well and which allowed him to range more widely than a purely academic career would have done. A life in academia, given the pressures to publish in specialised journals, might well have turned him into an economist who wrote mainly about a particular topic (such as pensions) and the broader Seldon view would have been lost – as would, of course, his publishing programme at the IEA, which was the source of much of the influence he wielded. The Institute gave him exactly the base he needed. In his position as Editorial Director, he was ideally placed not only to write himself but to formulate a programme of publications – to be written mainly by academic economists but carefully edited by him – with the specific purpose of explaining, in language that could be understood by those not technically trained in economics, the practical benefits of voluntary action in competitive markets, the virtues of self-help and the disadvantages of state intervention. In other words, he could carry forward the classical liberal economics he had learned at the LSE and transform it into a programme of action. Seldon saw his work at the IEA from the late 1950s onwards very much as a continuation of the work of the LSE economists of the 1930s.[14]

Two intellectual entrepreneurs

Seldon's publishing programme was at the heart of the success of the IEA, as Ralph Harris always acknowledged.[15] Interest in the IEA and the respective roles of Seldon and Harris[16] has been aroused because of the remarkable success of the Institute, which can reasonably be counted as the most influential think tank of the twentieth century, not only in Britain, where it was based, but possibly in the world because of the extent to which its influence spread. The Institute, established by Antony Fisher as explained above, and run from the mid-1950s to the late 1980s by Harris and Seldon, was quite different from the typical think tank of the early 21st century, which produces pamphlets and (occasional) bright ideas and is often associated with a particular political party. Searching for 'big ideas' is apparently the objective of these kinds of organisations. The IEA, however, was not searching: it knew what the 'big idea' was – a return to market liberalism – and wanted to explain how to achieve that goal.

Harris and Seldon were economists with similar ideas, not directly involved with any political party, who believed that the post-war consensus in favour of centralised planning and widespread government intervention was fundamentally wrong. As already explained, they were not concerned with marginal adjustments to that consensus. They wanted to overturn it, in the face of deep-rooted opposition. Eventually, after a long uphill battle against the establishment, their radical ideas for change triumphed: many of them were translated into practice by a sympathetic government and no subsequent government has so far reverted to the previous consensus. It can, of course, be argued that they were fortunate that a government receptive to their mode of thinking was elected in 1979. But the election of that government was not an independent event: one of the reasons for its election was the changed consensus that Harris and Seldon had begun to create.

These two intellectual entrepreneurs started work in the mid-1950s with very modest resources and in the most difficult of circumstances. They were advocates of market solutions and voluntary action, giving individuals the freedom to make decisions for themselves at a time when there was a near-universal belief that the 'planning' that had been successful in wartime could 'win the peace' also.[17] As Harris and Seldon wrote, in a book they co-authored which celebrated the first twenty years of the IEA,

> We set out to examine everything *ab initio*. Nothing was too sacred for economic analysis – from advertising and hire purchase, where we started, through fire, blood and water, to nuclear power, medical care, education, fuel, transport, broadcasting and pollution, even politics itself.[18]

To appreciate the obstacles they confronted, it is worth referring to the work of authors who have analysed the persistence of scientific paradigms.[19] It is very difficult in any field of knowledge to overturn a clear consensus that virtually everyone has come to accept. Huge vested interests build up which depend on maintenance of the consensus and which do everything they can to sustain it. The general message of the consensus is safe to convey in articles and speeches because few are likely to question it and it benefits from constant repetition. Criticism is dangerous because it often leads to the identification of the critic as a crank and it may mean that he or she is ridiculed.

One of the best analyses of this tendency to establish and maintain a consensus is by someone who was no friend of market liberalism. John Kenneth Galbraith, in *The Affluent Society*, conducts a very perceptive discussion of the issue. Galbraith coined the phrase 'the conventional wisdom', defining it as 'the name for the ideas which are esteemed at any time for their acceptability'. He pointed out that '... a very large part of our social comment – and nearly all that is well regarded – is devoted at any time to articulating the conventional wisdom'. The conventional wisdom, he said, is regarded as 'more or less identical with sound scholarship' and its position is 'virtually impregnable'.[20] Expression of the conventional wisdom is what nearly everyone wants to hear, and so it emerges in a stream of papers and speeches. Galbraith's analysis of the conventional wisdom neatly describes the collectivist consensus that Harris and Seldon faced in the 1950s, 1960s and 1970s.[21] What people wanted to hear was how government could solve this or that problem, and there was no shortage of 'intellectuals' prepared to tell them. They preferred not to listen to two economists who told them they should help themselves and let markets work. The conventional wisdom of that time about the benefits of collectivist 'solutions' seemed unassailable.

But Harris and Seldon, with a deep-seated belief in the power of the ideas they were putting forward, refused to accept the 'impregnability' of the other side's case. Their talents were complementary, as Chapter 7 explains in more detail. Seldon was the embodiment of intellectual rigour: Harris was an enthusiastic spreader of their message. Seldon was primarily a writer rather than a speaker, partly because of the stammer from which he suffered.[22] Harris was a witty and engaging speaker. In Milton Friedman's words, 'Ralph was a brilliant voice of the Institute; Arthur an unrelenting enforcer of academic standards in the Institute's books and the celebrated Hobart Papers he created'.[23] According to Ralph Harris, a 'natural division of labour' emerged: Seldon 'produced the goods' and Harris 'kept the shop'.[24] Harris was always generous in deferring to 'Arthur's intellectual pre-eminence'.[25] But one characteristic they had in common was sheer perseverance. It was that which allowed them to continue fighting for the best part of twenty-five years, which was the time it took before they made any real impact on a political and economic establishment that had, for many years, thought them to be cranks with views that had no relevance to the times in which they lived. Even after their views had started to be accepted, they were far from content. They continued to press for radical reforms, for instance of the welfare state, that went well beyond what the politicians of the day were willing to contemplate. Indeed, many of their proposed reforms are still not politically acceptable, even a decade into the 21st century.

5

Arthur Seldon's role in the IEA

Arthur Seldon's talents as an editor are widely acknowledged. He came to the Institute at a time when, as already explained, he and Ralph Harris were voices in the wilderness. One of the consequences was that it was difficult to persuade established authors to write for the Institute. Seldon realised that, if the IEA was to have influence, it must earn a reputation for clear yet intellectually rigorous analysis. He needed to recruit as authors talented economists and other social scientists, mainly from the universities, but initially such potential authors were reluctant to write for an institute that in its early days was little known and whose directors evidently had ideas far outside the mainstream economic and social wisdom of the day. Many potential authors probably feared that writing for such an organisation would damage their academic credibility.[1] In the early days, Seldon and Harris had to write many of the papers themselves, or occasionally in conjunction with others.

Gradually, however, the Institute began to establish a reputation, even though the intellectuals (the 'second hand dealers in ideas', as Hayek describes them) were unreceptive to market ideas, and the economics profession in particular was still overwhelmingly in the grip of Keynesian macroeconomics and interventionist ideas on microeconomic policy. In this hostile climate, Seldon and Harris patiently and unrelentingly explained the virtues of the price mechanism, not just as a matter of principle but in practice. The key element, in undertaking this difficult task and overcoming intellectual resistance, was the publishing programme devised by Seldon, which was designed to provide hard evidence that the price mechanism was superior to interventionist measures by government. Using the academic rigour he had learned at the LSE, allied with his practical experience of industry and commerce, he formulated this programme, recruited authors and edited their work to ensure that it would be understandable not just to economists but to a wider audience of intelligent laymen. In Ralph Harris's words, Seldon was the 'engine room' of the Institute.[2]

An essential part of Seldon's venture was the invention of a new form of publication. It was brief (often no more than 10,000 to 15,000 words), it was based on economic principles and, to the extent possible, it avoided technical jargon. Where technical terms were unavoidable, they were explained. Each publication was placed within a series ('Hobart Papers', 'Occasional Papers', 'Readings' etc.) depending on its length, the degree to which it contained original research and its other characteristics. The presence of a publication within a series indicated that it stood not on its own but as part of a more general view of the world.[3] Seldon's prefaces reinforced that view. He was adept at placing a particular paper within a more general context to show its relevance within the sphere of liberal market ideas.[4]

Another particularly important part of Seldon's enterprise was his insistence that IEA authors should, in making recommendations, disregard the 'politically impossible'. Many academic economists found it hard to detach themselves from the conventional wisdom of the day and so would confine any policy recommendations they made within what they thought contemporary politicians would be willing to accept. But Seldon realised that this attitude would suppress all ideas for radical reform, allowing the conventional wisdom to be constantly reinforced.

He therefore insisted that IEA authors should follow their arguments through to their logical conclusions in terms of recommendations for action, whether or not there seemed any chance of their implementation in the near future. Had Seldon not taken this approach, it is hard to see how the flow of radical ideas that came out of the IEA – on labour market reforms, inflation control, privatisation and so on – could then have emerged. It follows that, had there not been such a flow of ideas, the political agenda in Britain and other countries would not have changed as it did.[5] Rejection of the idea of conforming to the 'politically possible' was a key element in the Seldon philosophy, which led directly to the setting of an agenda for fundamental reform which was eventually, albeit imperfectly, translated into a programme of government action.

As Seldon gradually established the IEA's publishing programme, which was the essential source of its growing reputation, he began to attract some of the world's most eminent economists and other social scientists to write for the Institute. He did not confine himself to authors from the United Kingdom. One of his favoured recruiting grounds was the Mont Pelerin Society (MPS), in which both he and Harris were active, and where they met an international group of very distinguished scholars. Hayek, who had been instrumental in establishing the MPS in 1947,[6] had, as explained in Chapter 3, also been involved in the setting up of the Institute, and wrote a number of substantial papers for it. Seldon was always quick to recognise promising areas of research before their significance was widely accepted, and to import ideas, particularly from the United States. For instance, he foresaw the importance of Milton Friedman's work on monetary policy at a time when British governments were still involved in 'fiscal fine tuning': in 1970 the IEA brought Friedman to London to give a lecture on monetary economics which had a significant influence on future government policies.[7]

Seldon also saw the implications of public choice theory for the balance between state and voluntary activity: in 1978 the

IEA organised a conference on 'The Economics of Politics', at which another American economist, James Buchanan, one of the founding fathers of public choice, was among those who gave papers. Other comments on the influence of the public choice school on Seldon are in Chapter 11 below.

Another area in which Seldon was active was in searching for promising young academics, who were often recommended to him by their older colleagues. When he started the IEA's journal, *Economic Affairs*, in 1980, one of his purposes was to provide an outlet for relatively short publications by promising young academics and others with liberal market ideas who could begin their publishing careers in the journal.

Many authors have testified about Seldon's skill in editing manuscripts supplied by authors and how much time he spent on improving them.[8] Sometimes he was perhaps too interventionist in changing authors' words. His great ability, however, was to transform a paper written by an academic author into a readable paper which could be understood by most intelligent people, which ended with clear recommendations and which Seldon's preface placed within a more general liberal market agenda. As Gordon Tullock has said of Seldon's contribution to one of the IEA's most influential publications, *The Vote Motive*,

> Arthur Seldon did a spectacularly good job of editing. Indeed, he could almost be called co-author … Since Seldon did the same superb job of editing and practically rewriting many other IEA publications, he can claim to be a major influence in the improvement of economics and political science not only in England but also in the remainder of the English-speaking world.[9]

Hayek recognised the skill that Seldon had shown in editing the papers he had published via the IEA to the extent that, when he was concerned that ill health might prevent his finishing *Law, Legislation and Liberty*, he requested that, in such an event, Seldon should complete it for him.[10]

As the IEA's reputation grew, Seldon also drew into its publications – as authors, commentators or reviewers – people who were critical of liberal market ideas. Seldon was sufficiently confident in the robustness of these ideas that he was not afraid to include the views of opponents within the covers of IEA papers.[11] Moreover, he recognised the value of critics of IEA papers in giving authors new ideas and helping them to sharpen their analyses.

Seldon was a very dedicated editor who spent much of his working life, when he was not writing himself, thinking about the IEA's publishing programme and how it might be extended and improved. A striking example of how the Institute's publishing programme dominated his working life is to be found in a series of letters he wrote to Ralph Harris in August 1965. Seldon was on holiday in the Isle of Wight when he was diagnosed with a duodenal ulcer, which for a time made him seriously ill. During his confinement throughout much of August 1965 in the Royal Isle of Wight County Hospital in Ryde, he wrote a number of letters to Harris which the latter preserved and later passed on to Marjorie Seldon. The letters, which are reproduced below (not all precisely dated), are significant in revealing that Seldon was constantly thinking about his publishing programme and that he felt a great urge to return to his life's work. In Harris's words, '... they demonstrated his dedication to IEA work, even whilst under doctor's orders'.[12]

Letters to Ralph Harris from Arthur Seldon, sent from the Isle of Wight County Hospital in August 1965

9/11 August 1965

My Dear Ralph,
I was moved to a private ward on Friday and I get better nights, I am feeling stronger and better but I still shan't be allowed home until my blood count is back to

normal, and the Doctor says that will probably be two weeks. I'm trying to do nothing but the effort yields rapidly diminishing returns so I read light matter but I most enjoy good writing especially when it is used to convey worthwhile thoughts. And here your inspiration of bringing some of Stigler's work to me has been a Godsend. I'm sure he is twice as effective as he would have been if he had assailed the reader's ear with discordant cacophony.

We must try to reach even higher standards in the prose of everything we publish. Perhaps as the Institute grows in stature even eminent outside authors will be more ready to allow us to improve their writing. As I lie here thoughts come on what we might have done or should be doing on current problems. I think you probably have listed them yourself but some emerge from the exchange we had with the breakfast meeting with Maurice Macmillan and Scott Hopkins. I said that we took some pains to time our publications to have the maximum impact. They suggested we study the Queen's speeches to see what the Government intended. So these five or six I put down now are high on the list.

1) The National Plan, a third edition, as soon as possible after George Brown publishes on the 16th September. Will John Brunner be co-operative?
2) Second edition of *Land and the Market* to spike the Land Commission's proposals but dear old Donald needs some editing for his economic analysis is not his strong point.
3) We must have something really good and well informed and up to date on Housing. I don't know whether John Carmichael's Hobart can be re-fashioned (I doubt it) into the kind of study I have in mind. He does not really know enough about the institutional framework or about the financial

machinery. I wish we could do this one together –
you on housing for letting and me on housing for
sale. On my side I'm sure the whole of the Building
Society Acts will have to be reconstructed and this is
only one part of the subject.

4) A Hobart on short term financial, fiscal measures.

5) Further to my letters on Mass Observation I read the
figures. 23% of the sample who are not now privately
insured for medical services would contract out with
a £5 a head voucher and 30% (23% plus 9% of 76%)
with a £7 voucher and 15% of the sample who did
not pay school fees would take a £50 voucher. And
31%, (15% and 18% of 82%) a £100 voucher. These
groups must include many with modest salaries and
even with wage earnings. All this in addition to the
17% who insure privately for health (which must be
BUPA etc's 3 to 4, plus 12% of HSA, HSF etc.) and
the 6% to 8% of parents with children at fee paying
schools.

Now, as Nigel was saying, it would be difficult to
exaggerate the significance of these findings. They mean
that a large section of the public would prefer a service
different from that supplied by the state. What more
evidence do the politicians want to encourage them to
re-direct state welfare? I leave this to your unerring
tactical judgement.

You might send some copies of Haberler and Clarke
to Alan Watkins of *The Spectator* who might like to learn
about Liquidity and Sterling as a reserve currency. I'm
hoping that you will think about dealing with the
impending autumn impasse on the exchange reserves etc
but who? Journalists are too prone to deal with surface
symptoms and academics take too long. Can we persuade
Robbins or Paish, dare we risk Alan Day? Now that
Enoch is in defence can we re-activate Len Benton? I

had a long talk with him in 1963 in which I put a string of leading economic questions that he said he would work into his Hobart.

6) We need an Eaton paper on the meeting of markets between East and West. This is a strong card we should play more and more. That the East is turning to markets to get out of its mess and that we in the West should make more use of an instrument we have allowed to rust.

7) A Hobart on Trade Union Reconstruction. But who?

11 August 1965

Dear Ralph

I must be tiring you, you must have many pressing matters to attend to but I long to be back by your side. May I just mention a word of the other things that have come to my mind.

1) Maurice Wiggins, we must use him somewhere. Michael Joseph?

2) Desmond Donnelly, could we publish his book in the Michael Joseph series?

3) Jackson could take on Margaret Miller in *Observer* (marvellous!).

4) The doctors – re-publicise our stuff on medical services to encourage the independents who look like leaving the NHS in and around Brighton. You can't do everything but we want to be in touch with a Doctor Smith in Birmingham. This defection has come just at the right time to stimulate public and Conservative Central Office interest in the second welfare survey. I long to get back to help write interpretation and commentary.

5) Keith Joseph has not responded to my firmly worded letter. Is it worth finding out from him whether it is too late to change his recommendations to Heath? As they stand they are too weak although Jack Wiseman will assumingly defend them because he has assented to them. We shall lose twenty years if we cannot get the Conservatives to begin to de-nationalise social insurance. You are marvellous with people. Do you think you could try to have a word with KJ on the phone?

6) The new Individualism. A quick Hobart on economic policy, tax incentives, removal of obstacles to personal mobility etc. Or a short Michael Joseph book. Dare we let David Howell loose on this? He would have to agree to accept criticisms and suggestions on his contents. Or, best of all, Arnold Plant. For a magnum opus but he would want £750 or more.

We must knock social cost theory; Walter Taplin said Coase would definitely be getting in touch with us.

Peter's ms needs much strengthening.

Reynolds has the makings of a telling onslaught on Buchanan the town planner and all his works. The typescript seems to me to be 70% and we can get him, the author, to improve it to 80% or 85% and then at 85 we shall publish.

I don't see anyone else who is able or ready to do the job. Everyone else is either engaged or not just right.

Later

Dear Ralph,

How gracious of Enoch to ask about me. Please thank him for his good wishes. I never seemed to hit it off with him. You handle him beautifully, and he must be most grateful to you for this. I hope he won't resent Seale's essay on doctors in the Eaton Paper.

I imagine that Hamish has all these ms's under control. Anyway, grateful thanks for coming to see me and for comforting Marjorie. Love to you, José and the children.

[Undated]

Dear Ralph,

The chances are that I shall be about home either next Friday [20th August] or the following Tuesday [24th August]. I shall then be ready to receive you at Otford for preliminary drafting. This time we two should both sign it *Choice in Welfare Mark II*. With luck we might prepare a penultimate ms by the following week, say Wednesday, 1st September. I don't know whether it's worth getting one or two quick second opinions? We should not want to keep it too late and we should publish the report in good time on say Friday, 17th September.

We must avoid being swamped by the national plan on the 15th. On the other hand *Choice in Welfare II* will be highly dramatic. It will be fact, not fortune-telling fiction. We should also look at the dates of the Party conferences.

2) The doctor says I must convalesce for at least two weeks after returning home that brings me to mid September and Michael's wedding in Yorkshire which I'd like to travel to on the 25th September.

Thank you for your letter to KJ. It showed your masterly, tactical skill. But again you credit me with advocacy which you yourself have buttressed and re-inforced at every point. If we indeed can induce the Conservatives to begin removing compulsory National

Insurance, which they must, then we shall share the same satisfaction of inducing politicians to combine courage with foresight.

I have sent Joseph one short comment on his letter he may refer to you, if you see him next week. I'm fairly firm in the letter because I felt that we must speak plainly without circumlocution.

Tell him that I have taken you, and only you, into my confidence about criticisms of his policy proposals. Excellent idea to send him some of the Mass Observation tables. He will be especially interested in the proportion of people who are moving privately to pension schemes and other ways. Important in view of the proposal for the obligatory second private pension.

And now I must tell you of my personal condition. The hospital matron, when I asked how soon I could leave, said that when I came in I was very ill. She used the words 'you were over the top'. I haven't told Marjorie this. But that I was getting better and would recover slowly. This left me some sober reflection for an hour. The ulcer is not in itself fatal or dangerous but what was surprising to the doctors was my reaction to it which they say reflected a lack of physical robustness. I don't know how much of that is the talk of overdoing it and how much is my own restless temperament but I'm resolved to reducing the demand on my physical resources. And, that means cutting out everything outside of the Institute. I'm saying no to Napper Stinton Consultancy, the university examining, no to invitations to write for anything except national newspapers, I'm saying no to Tim Raison, I'm stopping the *Building Society Gazette* quarterly articles and anything else I'm committed to.

And I'm going to ask you please to consider salaries. It is difficult for me to say this but I will. I should go up to five thousand from January and you to more than five thousand five hundred. Please also think of ways in which we can build up capital as well as tax income.

Will McEwan Younger give us some shares? You and I should be entirely relieved of money manipulations to enable us to do our best work for the Institute and all it could do. Please think about this and let me have your feelings.

[Undated]

My Dear Ralph,
Procedure for Monday 23rd August
I'm compiling thoughts and notes for sections, paragraphs and sentences etc but will it not burden you to take them all down, work on them, and dictate them on Tuesday? We can then have them typed out on Wednesday and returned to Otford on Thursday. Do you think we should have a secretariat?

And we must do something to weaken the influence of the NIESR [National Institute of Economic and Social Research]. This morning's stuff, about it saying the balance of payment deficiency can be wiped out at the end of next year is not economic analysis but necromancy, bogus stuff, nonsense. Who can we get to dissect these forecasts? I'm writing to Richard Fry – he's always been very critical of the NIESR.

I probably will not feel like doing intensive drafting and it will be a big drain on you if you have to do it all yourself. We have to have the first draft completed before you go to Stresa and we should have a second meeting too say Thursday 26th.
As ever,
Arthur

[Undated]

Dear Ralph,
You should have medical checks twice a year. Your
general health seems robust but your output is larger than
that of almost any man I have known. Sorry to mention
it but you are now in your fifth decade and without over
sentimentality we have a duty to our families as well as to
our philosophies and we shan't help our philosophy by
breaking up our health. Don't chide me for writing at
some length. If Joan types it out it will seem much
shorter.

 I lie here patiently and my heart is with Marjorie and
I yearn to be at my desk.
 Yours ever,
 Arthur

 Another consequence of the Isle of Wight episode occurred
a few years later and again demonstrates how Seldon was always
thinking about cases where markets needed to be established
and about the IEA's publishing programme. In 1968, he was
advised by his specialist, Dr Southwell, to have an operation on
the ulcer to avoid its bursting. Marjorie Seldon recalls that,
because of an oversight before the operation, the small Catholic
hospital near Vauxhall where he was being treated failed to test
his blood.[13] When he had a haemorrhage after the operation, it
turned into a life-threatening crisis because the hospital discovered that he had a rare blood type which was not readily available. Eventually, a donor (a bus conductor in Edgware) was
found in time to save his life. It is not surprising that the episode
left a deep impression on Seldon, but it is typical of him that
afterwards, as he pondered on his experience, he began to consider the economic implications of the deficiency in blood
supply he had encountered. As a consequence, he commissioned
one of the IEA's most controversial papers, *The Price of Blood*,[14]
which argued the case for establishing a market in blood in

which donors would be paid and which might avoid the kind of shortage that had threatened his life.[15]

To summarise Arthur Seldon's role at the IEA, his own description, in the last preface he wrote just before he retired from active involvement with the Institute, can hardly be bettered:

> In choosing authors for IEA papers over 30 years, often with the assistance of the academic advisers, I sometimes felt like the manager of a cricket team putting the best players in to 'bat' against the opposing sides. Historians will judge the effects of the long academic debate on public and political opinion, as seen in the intellectual and cultural revolution between the 1950s, when the market was anathema, and the 1980s, when it is being offered by every political party, old and new ...[16]

6

The Harris–Seldon partnership: working together and its problems

The Isle of Wight letters, as well as emphasising Seldon's dedication to his role at the IEA, demonstrate the warmth of the relationship between him and Ralph Harris in the mid-1960s, after they had been working together for about eight years. Seldon even devotes one of his letters from hospital (the last) to advising Harris to safeguard his own health. The relationship was clearly much more than one between two people who happened to be working in the same office. They were close friends who were working in pursuit of a common objective. As Harris expresses it, '… on good days or bad, I increasingly found myself looking on Arthur as a second brother with whom it would be inconceivable to fall out very seriously or for very long'. He and Arthur, in his words, '… cheerfully withstood our share of problems and anxieties, and more than our share of opposition'.[1]

The working partnership between these two friends who had such success in changing public opinion was one between two people with complementary skills. Their respective roles in the Institute evolved in the light of experience rather than being set down in an organisation chart. Seldon worked away in the back room, in charge of the product and producing a stream of high-quality yet readable papers about important economic and social issues. Harris was the outgoing frontman, the public face of the IEA, who presented that product to the world. Harris attributed their close and productive relationship not only to their 'intellectual bonds' and their 'missionary dedication' to the IEA's work, but also to their 'common origins among the aspiring working classes of North and East London'.[2]

Nevertheless, despite this warmth, the complementarity between Harris and Seldon and the remarkable results they achieved, it is hardly surprising that, in a 30-year partnership, from time to time tensions arose. Some were continuing, but minor. As Ralph Harris has explained, Seldon was occasionally concerned that Harris's activities outside the Institute (for example, setting up the Wincott Foundation, campaigning against grammar school closures and acting as secretary of the Mont Pelerin Society) were taking up too much of his time and diverting them from what they should be doing. Harris's tight control of the Institute's finances also occasionally irritated Seldon.[3] But there were at least two more serious issues, both of which have been acknowledged by Harris. The first stemmed from an action by Harris which had consequences he did not intend. The second arose from an action by the Thatcher government.

The first, and the more serious, of these problems in the partnership arose in 1968 (three years after the Isle of Wight letters) when, in a move intended to strengthen the Institute, Harris appointed John Wood as its Deputy Director. Seldon, who was impressed neither by Wood's ability as an economist nor by the contribution he could make to the work of the Institute, thought that the appointment of Wood must, at least by implication, diminish his own role in the Institute and make him appear inferior to Harris's 'Deputy'. For a time, Seldon felt considerable resentment and the old warmth seemed to disappear. The strength of his feeling can be seen in the following recollection by Marjorie Seldon of the genesis of the 'third man' problem and its consequences.

Marjorie Seldon's view of 'the third man'

The work of the Institute under Arthur's editorship was becoming recognised in other parts of the world as well as the UK so he was invited to visit Australia to discuss welfare issues with Government Ministers in 1968. During his absence of some weeks, Ralph decided to ask an old friend of his, John Wood who was then out of work, to join the IEA as Deputy Director. Ralph did this in all innocence, motivated by a desire to help out a friend, and believing Arthur would welcome another economist to 'the team'. Up to this time Ralph and Arthur had formed a highly complementary and indeed affectionate relationship. As many recognised, Arthur 'put the books on the shelves' and Ralph 'sold them'. It was some time before Ralph realised that he had 'put a spanner in the works'.

It wasn't in Arthur's character to voice his annoyance but it dawned on Ralph, who knew him so well, that Arthur had developed a frosty manner, not only to John Wood but, to Ralph's dismay, himself as well. In an attempt to mollify Arthur, Ralph rationalised it would be useful to have a public school man with an upper class manner beside the 'two working class lads' at lunches and other fund raising events. To do Ralph justice, Arthur had never enjoyed those events and was always anxious to return to his desk while Ralph was still engaged in trying to get sizeable donations from the guest or guests.

It was no help to Ralph in his efforts to persuade Arthur to accept John Wood as a partner, that John was not a hard worker. That said, it has to be recognised that it would have made no difference if John had tried to help Arthur with the publications. Not only did Arthur resent any input from John, feeling as he did that John had been foisted on him, but Arthur did not believe John

was a true classical liberal economist. Arthur had been
schooled under Friedrich von Hayek, Lionel Robbins
and Arnold Plant at the London School of Economics:
he believed to his core in the moral and practical
economic tenet that people will invariably get better
value with their own money than Governments spending
it for them.

John did co-operate with Robert Miller in writing
two publications[4] but Arthur remained hostile. Realising
this, Ralph wrote to the editor of *The Times* asking if
they had a place for a good economist (which John was)
but no offer was made and John remained at the IEA.

Arthur had started taking one day a week at home
which he found useful with his own writing, and editing
contributions from external economists without
interruptions. Ralph had also found one day at home
useful in preparing stratagems to raise money. What he
did not expect was that Arthur began to arrange to stay
at home on the days that he knew Ralph would be in
the office. Of course they spoke on the telephone but for
several months they were not in the office together as
frequently as they had previously been. Since the advent
of John, Arthur had several times contemplated resigning
from the IEA and finding another job. What prevented
him doing so was certainly not the IEA salary, for neither
he nor Ralph earned what they could both have done
elsewhere.

To Ralph's relief, Arthur eventually decided that for
the sake of the mission for which they had founded the
Institute, he must do his best to accept John's presence in
the office. Ralph happily assumed that he and Arthur and
John would tolerate each other without any friction. He
would refer to the 'three musketeers' and other remarks
to give visitors to the office the impression that the three
of them were equally productive, but it was too much for
Arthur when an American photographer arrived to

photograph the three together. He walked into his office and shut the door. There was no photograph that day.

For the years until John's premature death, Ralph and Arthur worked together as they had in the early years. There was much affection for Arthur from Ralph but it was never the visible warmth between them as in the pre John Wood years.

This episode is also described by Ralph Harris is his 'Living with Arthur', where he accepts that Seldon had reasonable cause for concern about John Wood's 'leisurely, even lethargic, mode of work'. Indeed, Harris says he urged Wood to 'throw himself more energetically into a specific piece of research or writing'.[5] Harris, however, did not feel, as does Marjorie Seldon, that there was never again the 'visible warmth' between the two men that had previously existed. Whatever the feelings of the two men may have been, there seems to have been at least a temporary period of strained relations during which the effectiveness of their working relationship – which Harris compared to that of Gilbert and Sullivan – may have been disturbed. Nevertheless, it seems not to have been long before, as Marjorie Seldon explains, Arthur decided that the 'third man' episode could not be allowed to interrupt the vital work that he and Harris had still to do.

Eleven years later, in 1979, another problem emerged, this time as a consequence of outside forces. The incoming Thatcher government raised Ralph Harris to the peerage (as Lord Harris of High Cross) but gave no corresponding honour to Arthur Seldon. Inevitably, this action suggested to the outside world that Harris was the more important member of the partnership. It was an insensitive act by a government that recognised its debt to the IEA, but apparently failed to acknowledge that much of that debt was to Arthur Seldon's publishing programme, which formed the basis of the Institute's work and many of the ideas that the new administration put into practice.[6]

Harris himself, who had always acknowledged Seldon's role as the intellectual powerhouse of the Institute, was somewhat embarrassed that he had been singled out in this way. As he wrote some years after the event,

> ... I found his subtle exposition of the unsuspected light shed by theoretical analysis filled in gaps left by my abbreviated two-year post-war degree at Cambridge. When the least doubt about some aspect of our lonely free market mission flickered across my mind, it did not survive what can only be described as my continuous seminar with Arthur ... Never off-duty, he was always ready with fertile, unwavering answers for every challenge thrown at us.[7]

And, specifically on the peerage,

> ... I recognised and deferred to Arthur's intellectual pre-eminence as the essential ingredient in the growing reputation won by the IEA, not least among the ranks of Tuscany which he was earlier than me to cultivate. All the more, I saw my peerage in 1979 as a possible threat to our flourishing partnership ... I felt, and have to this day continued to feel an acute sense of the gross inequity of being thus singled out for recognition of so conspicuously shared an achievement.[8]

Writing of Arthur and his wife, Marjorie, Harris says, '... it still angers me that these two incomparable champions of all that was best in Thatcherism should never have received the full public acknowledgement they both so richly merited'.[9]

In 1983, Seldon was awarded a CBE (Commander of the Order of the British Empire) but the honour was not comparable to what Harris had received. Thereafter, Harris made considerable efforts, through his political contacts, to have Arthur Seldon's achievements recognised by the award of a knighthood. There were plenty of academic awards (see Appendix 2), but further recognition by the political establishment did not come.

As in the 'third man' case, however, Harris felt that, in the event, the partnership was not much affected by his peerage and that his close friendship with Arthur continued. As noted above, he wrote that he thought of Arthur as a 'second brother' and he said, also of the peerage, that 'I count it not the least of my blessings that our long friendship has survived and deepened, despite this potentially divisive contrast of unequal recognition'.[10]

Whatever damage may have been done by the 'third man' and peerage episodes, and whether or not the personal friendship cooled somewhat in the later years, it is clear that the working partnership remained fruitful to the end. Arthur Seldon, having begun his work at the IEA in 1957, remained there until late 1988.[11] In 1999, reflecting on the long partnership, he said that any differences between him and Harris had never been more than ones of emphasis. He said then of Harris,

> I spent most of my working life with this man for thirty years, and we bounce off each other. He always made me think harder about some things I was teaching and thinking at the time. I suppose unless there was a basic sympathy of outlook and hope it would have been difficult for two men to have lived and worked together in sympathy, with the occasional difference of emphasis, not difference of thought as it were, but difference of emphasis.[12]

PART III

LIVING AND WORKING
WITH ARTHUR SELDON

7

Family life

It will be obvious from Parts I and II of this book that Arthur Seldon was intensely interested in and involved with his work and that, to accomplish so much, he must have worked very long hours. He was not the conventional father, spending long hours at play with his children. He did not, however, neglect family life, and it is clear from his sons' recollections that he was devoted to them and, in particular, to helping them further their education and their own careers. Indeed, Arthur's upbringing in the East End Jewish community produced in him a strong family orientation: he felt very powerful family ties to his brothers and sister to whom, as explained in Chapter 1, he did not know he was so closely related until he was eleven, and to his mother, Eva Marks, who had brought him up with such love, care and personal sacrifice. When he and Marjorie had three children of their own, the five of them formed a close-knit family unit.

Marjorie's influence

As explained at the end of Chapter 1, Arthur and Marjorie married in secret in 1948, when Arthur was 32 and Marjorie was 29, because of their fears that Marjorie would not be accepted by Arthur's mother. Once they were married, however, such problems were gradually left behind them and the Seldons came to enjoy the support of Mrs Marks in their family life. Mrs Marks is remembered by the children as an affectionate grandmother, albeit rather severe looking, always dressed in black, and with a heavy East European accent.

Arthur and Marjorie were married for 57 years and clearly enjoyed a harmonious and understanding relationship which provided a stable and loving environment for their sons. In their relationship Marjorie was much more than the 'traditional' wife and mother, commonly found in the 25 years or so after World War II. She was Arthur's intellectual companion, not just assisting him by looking after the boys and running the household, but participating in his adventures in ideas. She understood and fully appreciated what he was trying to accomplish in his work at the IEA and in his writings, and she was an enthusiastic supporter of and accomplice in his (eventually successful) attempt to change the climate of opinion. Indeed, in some of his activities, such as the proposal to introduce an education voucher, she played a major part. In that case, she chaired a group called Friends of the Education Voucher Experiment in Representative Regions (FEVER), which tried to gather support for the voucher.[1] Marjorie was also very keen on the Mont Pelerin Society, attending its sessions rather than going along to meetings as a spouse, and she achieved the very rare distinction of becoming an MPS member in her own right.

More generally, Marjorie was someone on whom Arthur could try his ideas, knowing that he would have a sympathetic yet critical audience. Her intellectual support was crucial to his success. As Arthur recognised, he could not have accomplished what he did without her. Towards the end of his life, Marjorie had to go into hospital to have a hip operation. After she had been there for some time, during one of Arthur's visits he said to her, 'When are you coming home? I can't live without you.' His second sentence was quite literally true. Their interests and their lives were so intertwined that, to him, life without her was inconceivable.

The views of the boys

The Seldons' boys all grew up to admire their father and to recognise his strengths, even if he, even more than Marjorie, differed from the type of parent traditional in 1950s and 1960s Britain when they were growing up. Of course, like everyone else, he had weaknesses as a parent. In the words of Anthony, the Seldons' youngest son, Arthur was 'not exactly a roll-up-your-sleeves and get stuck into the playpit kind of dad. His mind was on higher things'. Nevertheless, the sons all remember him as a warm and loving father who, devoted to his work though he was, had time to advise and encourage each of them to find his own way in life and to help each to do so without imposing his own ideas. The quotations in the rest of this chapter are all from notes written by the three sons in private communications, or from their tributes at Arthur's memorial service.

Michael, who was Marjorie's son, adopted during her brief wartime marriage to Rex Perrott (who died in 1945), was the oldest child. He was five at the time of Arthur and Marjorie's marriage and was adopted by Arthur. The relationship between the new husband/stepfather and stepson could have been awkward but, in practice, it never seems to have been so, and Michael recalls that Arthur always treated him in exactly the same way as his two stepbrothers. Michael remembers Arthur as initially rather shy and believes that they were both uncertain

> … how we were going to manage this new relationship which neither of us had planned, and yet was for life. He let the relationship grow naturally, without forcing his ideas on me and yet I knew that his benign influence was always there in the background. His affection for my mother and loyalty to her was unbounded and the depth of their relationship created a stable and nurturing background to my formative years.

Arthur and Marjorie then had two sons, Peter, who was born

in February 1951, and Anthony, who was born in August 1953. Not surprisingly, given the intellectual bent of both parents, one of their principal concerns was with the boys' education, and they devoted considerable time to deciding what form of schooling would be most suitable. Peter recalls, of his father, that

> He would talk for many hours with my mother about whether this school or that was more suitable for each of us. Anthony was moved from Dulwich College Preparatory School to Bickley Park because it was deemed more suitable, and I was moved from being a day boy at Dulwich Prep to a full boarder aged ten until I left at thirteen. When Michael left Dulwich at thirteen, he was moved from a day boy to a boarder at Blundells in Tiverton, Devon.

It is also not surprising, given Seldon's upbringing and his views about voluntary provision, that he and Marjorie should decide to send their children to private schools, despite the financial sacrifices that had to be made by a family where earnings from work, based on an IEA salary with occasional earnings from elsewhere, were never high.

Anthony remembers 'his determination to pay for his three sons at private school – which involved real sacrifice and hardship', and Peter recalls,

> In all cases major spending sacrifices had to be made so that private school fees for all of us could be funded: a very old Rover 14 was kept until 1957 which had a permanent leak at the rear of the sunshine roof, and would regularly boil going up any kind of hill. Foreign holidays were out until our first in 1959 to Holland. Dad and Mum would rarely buy new clothes: Anthony asked his mother in about 1960 why she continued to wear her old red coat. But the latest clothes, and indeed any kind of 'nod' towards fashion held no interest for either of them.

Despite the care that the Seldons devoted to selecting the right schools, Peter was not a great achiever in academic terms. He recalls that, though his father must have been puzzled about and disappointed by his lack of progress at his secondary school, Sevenoaks, he never showed it.

> I believe he wanted to understand why an apparently intelligent son wasn't doing well at his school work, and eventually concluded (correctly) that it was primarily and simply a lack of motivation/interest in the subjects – and also the personal discipline to knuckle down to it!
>
> Dad's decision that I needed the regular academic routine of boarding life was almost certainly the right one in that I produced good results in my final years at prep school before going 'down hill academically' as a day boy at Sevenoaks.

If Arthur was disappointed with Peter's school performance, he must have been delighted in later years as Peter turned out to be a very successful entrepreneur, becoming an example of what Arthur termed, in one of his best IEA book titles, a 'prime mover of progress'.[2]

Despite his involvement in family life, Arthur was not 'domesticated'. He was not the kind of husband who performs duties in the kitchen and willingly undertakes all kinds of gardening and DIY jobs. According to Michael,

> As my mother uncomplainingly accepted, he was useless round the house. He could barely boil an egg, for his mind was elsewhere. The spirit was sometimes willing but the execution was beyond him. He occasionally harboured the fond idea that he could do little jobs around the place, like putting up a shelf, and he armed himself with racks of hand tools, none of which he ever mastered. One of these was a screwdriver that was meant to work round corners. This was not only completely

outside his own realm of comprehension but also baffled everyone else that laid eyes on it.

His dress sense also tended towards the formal. In Peter's words,

> I remember that Dad was an intensely organised and tidy man: everything had its place. He was always very well groomed with his combed back, shiny jet black hair, and despite his old suits always looked smart in his 'office' clothes. His casual clothes sense was less sure footed, and in truth he was more comfortable in a shirt and tie, if not a jacket most of the time. Anthony and I well remember him helping us build sand castles on the beach in the Scilly Isles wearing dark flannels, a white shirt and a tie!

The priority the Seldons placed on educating their sons limited their funds for other family activities. Nevertheless, they always had family holidays. As Anthony says, 'He always took us for family holidays, even when money was scarce. A farm in South Devon was the destination. He would work while watching us play, an indulgent smile on his face.' And, 'He was always exceptionally generous. When shopping for the latest bit of Scalextric kit, he would start humming the Volga boat song very loudly if he thought the latest cars were too expensive. But pay he did.'

In addition to his work, Arthur had an interest in cricket, which, as all the boys recall, he would play with them on the lawn. In Michael's words,

> Cricket was what continued to interest him. He couldn't play because of his stiff elbow and ankle, the result of a disease of the joints which he contracted during his war service, but he could still be persuaded to bowl spinners to me in the garden. 'Ah-ha!' he would say when I played and missed.[3]

Arthur Seldon's principal interests, however, were ideas —
reading the literature of economics, writing the many books and
papers that he produced and editing the work of the authors
that he brought together so effectively in the IEA's publishing
programme. Inevitably, therefore, much of his time at home was
spent in work. Michael says,

> We did not see a lot of him at home, not that he wasn't
> there but because he was so often working in 'the study'.
> His commitment to his work was striking. In the early
> years he used to supplement his regular income by
> marking economics exam papers ('scripts' as he called
> them) but later his fertile mind was more in demand
> from the wider world of his profession.

His editorial instincts were deep rooted. He always read with
pen in hand, ready to correct infelicities of English expression or
lack of clarity, whether in books, newspapers or journal articles.
Anthony remembers his father's last visits to Wellington College,
where Anthony is headmaster: 'The last two times I saw him, he
was poring over a brochure from Wellington College, a happy
man, apart from some of the English in the brochure, which he
edited heavily. He was an editor to the end.'

Children are, of course, often unaware of their parents' qualities in their professional lives but Arthur's sons all grew up to
realise that their father was a great thinker. Michael sums up his
qualities as

> He was a lion among thinkers, fearless and untiring. His
> eminence as an economist was, I think, due not only to
> his outstanding intellect and application, but also, and
> perhaps far more importantly, to his compassion. Among
> his many memorable qualities one that I continue to
> recall with great admiration is that he always seemed to
> be more interested in promoting ideas that he felt would
> be of benefit to the world than he was in being

recognised as the author of or contributor to them.

And Peter saw in his father the effects of his East End background:

> I feel Dad's impatience, and certainly his restlessness to get on with his evangelising work, was born of the self reliance he saw around him and experienced in his formative years in the East End.

> The combination of this background and his humanist instincts informed and shaped his thinking to the core. For all his genius he was a profoundly wise, kind, and modest man who was determined that 'ordinary people' should be empowered and liberated through the choice markets create, and the personal dignity they confer on individuals as customers, not mere recipients of below standard, 'one size fits all', public services ... there wasn't an ounce of pomposity in him – in sharp contrast to so many other eminent people I have met over the years.

Michael echoes Peter's sentiments about their father's personality:

> I learned many things from my stepfather, and one of the most important lessons he taught me, not in words but by example, was the way in which he never tried to be anyone other than who he truly was. As he grew in academic stature, as he became known more and more widely, as his name became synonymous with fair minded and clearly expressed ideas powerfully and effectively delivered, his manner remained as self-effacing as ever. He didn't change at all.

Anthony's case is particularly interesting, because he became a teacher, headmaster and political historian and biographer,[4] following quite closely in his father's footsteps as an intellectual. Anthony recognises that 'Having an intellectual as a father was sometimes a mixed blessing. There was always a sense of "other worldliness" about him … His intellect penetrated deep and far into economics, into politics and philosophy'.

He would engage the boys in discussions about current events. Anthony recalls that

> As the 1960s went on, I became increasingly aware of his view that the world was divided between the bad guys – communists, socialists and old style Tories – and the good guys who believed in something called the free market – a bit difficult for a teenager to grasp.

But his father was a great example to him and encouraged him in whatever he did.

> Facts were what interested him, not fiction and imagination. I never knew him read a novel, a poem or a play. Yet he sat through endless plays I directed at Oxford and beyond … He encouraged me to found my own Institute. He helped me believe in myself.

His father influenced Anthony's choice of A-level subjects, and helped him to achieve A grades in economics and politics by teaching him and lending him relevant books. Anthony's decision to read PPE at Oxford was again influenced by his father – though he later regretted that he had not read history instead since, in his words, 'I never really understood either philosophy or economics'. Economics did not 'wow' Anthony in the way it did Arthur, which Anthony thinks was always a matter of regret to his father.

Anthony's decision to write a doctorate was also a result of encouragement by his father, though at that stage he had switched from economics to contemporary history. The thesis was turned into Anthony's first book, to Arthur's delight. 'He was thrilled when I turned it into my first book in 1981. Now, he felt, I had arrived. He was not thrilled ... by my decision to become a school teacher, though he happily went along with it, and was pleased by the various successes that cropped up from time to time along the way.'

When, later, Anthony started the Institute of Contemporary British History in 1987, his father was very engaged with what he was trying to do. In retrospect, Anthony thinks, '... it was replicating the IEA'.

The three boys were all immensely proud of their father, both because of his personal qualities and because of his great achievements. They accepted whatever parental failings he had, recognising that they were a consequence of his dedication to a worthy mission in life and that they had an outstanding individual for a father. Anthony expressed their view particularly well in the tribute he paid at his father's memorial service: 'He was a singular man. A romantic. A man of powerful emotions he rarely let the world see, or himself indulge in.'

8

Working with
Arthur Seldon

Martin Anderson worked with Arthur Seldon at the IEA from 1977 to 1987, during which time, despite Martin's lack of formal training in economics, Seldon helped him to become a skilled editor and had him appointed editor of the IEA's journal, Economic Affairs. *In Martin's words, 'he shaped me in his own image'. Seldon may well have seen Martin as an eventual successor. But when the incoming regime at the IEA made it clear that no such succession was likely, the attractions of a much better-paid job at the Organisation for Economic Cooperation and Development (OECD) in Paris became obvious and Martin left. His recollections here of the man are particularly enlightening because of his close working relationship with Arthur Seldon.*

Working with Arthur Seldon was an education and a joy. The proselytising zeal that animated his work as an editor and writer made him an instinctive teacher: he exuded a passion for communicating the truths in which he believed, and did so with unflagging energy. If his career had taken a different turn, he could have been a teacher, a journalist, a film-maker: one can imagine him active in any number of media. Indeed, he embraced new means of communication as they presented themselves: his own work precluded much direct involvement when the IEA began to record videos but he was an enthusiastic adviser to Anthony Jay and Jonathan Lynn when they were preparing the scripts of *Yes Minister*, beginning in 1980. Arthur's *The Riddle of the Voucher*[1] – which examined how vested interests in the Department of Education and Science were able to thwart the aims of a well-intentioned minister[2] and scupper the proposed introduction of the education voucher – tells essentially the same story in academic language, but Arthur was delighted to help satire bring his message to a far wider audience than he would ever reach.

Arthur's effectiveness in formulating the IEA 'message', which transformed the climate of opinion in Britain and abroad, is the more remarkable when one realises that he was galvanising disparate bodies of thought. The free-market movement, nationally and internationally, is a complex mix of Christian absolutists and libertarian relativists, of economists of both the Chicago and Vienna schools, differing in whether they see the world in terms of 'perfect competition' and equilibrium or of markets in constant, chaotic turmoil. There are differences, too, in the extent to which free marketeers feel comfortable in becoming involved in politics. The tensions inherent in this movement were a feature of life inside the IEA, too: its two leading lights sat on either side of a divide. Ralph Harris, who was happy to characterise himself as a 'Christian gentleman', had been a Liberal Unionist candidate in the 1951 election and a Conservative one in 1955 and enjoyed mixing with politicians; he was the classic 'joiner', the gladhander, the perfect frontman for the Institute. Arthur, whom I never once heard mention his Jewish background, had dallied with the Liberal Party, of course, but had long since put political engagement behind him; he found many of the visitors to the IEA lunches tiresome and saw no reason to curry favour with the politicians who darkened our doorstep[3] – he was much happier upstairs in his office, engaged in extended debate with his authors.

But he understood that the arguments in favour of the market economy bridged a continuum from high-church Tories to radical libertarians, and he possessed an uncanny ability to state his own fundamentally radical views in a way that would not only not excite the antagonism of the more conservative parts of his audience but even encourage their eager agreement. I witnessed this acuity of judgement at work on countless occasions, none more skilfully than during the Mont Pelerin Society meeting at Cannes in 1994. Speaker after speaker had come forward to say how lucky we were to have government after government implementing free-market policies around the world. Arthur, for whom the glass of liberty was always half empty, stood up from the floor and said, with some passion, that this reliance on the state to push through a liberalising reform agenda was misplaced: 'If we wait for governments to give us what we want, we'll never get it.' The room promptly erupted in applause – for an argument far more radical than most of those present would have knowingly endorsed. I asked him afterwards whether he had intended to express himself quite so starkly; yes, he said, although he realised that the thrust of his argument would have escaped some of his listeners. Meantime, the thought had been planted in their minds.

First encounters with Arthur and the IEA

My first direct contact with Arthur had come not quite twenty years earlier, at St Andrews, where in the autumn of 1976 I began the last year of the course that would lead to an MA in medieval French and German. Aside from a passing acquaintance with a handful of IEA publications, my knowledge of economics was sketchy, and my libertarianism instinctive rather than informed. But I had been a member of the solidly free market Conservative Association at the university since my student days began three years earlier, and that September, having arrived back in St Andrews after a summer term abroad, I was one of a handful of students – all fellow members of the Conservative Association – who ran around at a gathering of the Mont Pelerin Society. It had been convened in St Andrews because of the proximity of the town to Kirkcaldy, birthplace of Adam Smith, 1976 being the bicentenary of the publication of *The Wealth of Nations* – and because of Ralph Harris's fondness for the place: he had lectured in political economy there from 1949 to 1956.

The tasks for us red-gowned helpers were hardly onerous. We manned a fleet of minibuses to pick up MPS members from Edinburgh airport and return them a week later. We had to get copies made – by the hundred – of papers often delivered at the last moment. And there were a myriad other small tasks to do. We were all volunteers, but the thrill of meeting some of the minds directly responsible for our worldview was compensation enough. Acting as our visitors' guides to St Andrews and its colourful history was a true pleasure, though at the time I don't think I appreciated that walking round the town lecturing to a group that included Milton and Rose Friedman was something of a privilege.[4]

At the time, of course, I had no idea that this week in St Andrews was acquainting me with many of the personalities who were to people my career, shape my views, become friends and – in Arthur's case – become a beloved father-figure and one of the two most influential figures in my own thinking. My efforts during those seminal six days can't have created too bad an impression: when in May the next year word came up to St Andrews that the IEA was looking for a general factotum, I rang Ralph Harris to ask about the job; I was asked in turn when I could start. Turning my back on life as a philologist, I left St Andrews on 11 June 1977, a Saturday, to begin work the next Monday; when on the train south on the Sunday I read an extended and enthusiastic review in the *Sunday Telegraph* of Milton Friedman's *Inflation and Unemployment: The New Dimension of Politics*, the IEA's Occasional Paper 51, to be published the next morning, I was both proud and depressed – happy to be working for an organisation that could command such attention, but disheartened because one of my duties was to send out the post, and I now knew how I was going to be spending the next afternoon.

My job, in fact, was that of an elevated gopher. It had been occupied before me by Chris Tame, whose outline of Arthur's early life is one of the principal bases for Chapter 1 of this book. Chris had initiated a programme to mail all the teachers of A-level and Higher Economics in the country, to encourage them to subscribe to IEA publications; I took it over and completed it. I proofread the three-foot-long swirls of the galleys of books that Mike Solly, the Publications Manager, was seeing through publication. These and sundry other tasks didn't require me to report to Arthur directly, but he could see that I was an under-exploited resource and began to make use of me. He found it especially useful that I had a formal training in languages and started passing me his own articles for my reaction: to catch the odd grammatical transgression and to see whether I could sharpen his argument – perhaps, too, given my lack of formal training in economics, to be sure that his points had come across.

Working with Arthur was by far the most interesting part of my early life at the IEA. And that passionate drive to communicate meant that mere proximity to him was an education. To begin with, I had a desk in the library, opposite that of Ken Smith, the librarian. It was the perfect position. Visitors, distinguished and otherwise, would come in to chat. Spontaneous seminars would develop, with them or other members of the staff. And for Arthur the library was an impromptu lecture theatre. Once he had finished in the office for the day, he would come down the stairs and, ostensibly to kill time before setting off to catch the next train to Sevenoaks, would walk up and down the library, letting off steam with Ken and me about the latest government idiocy or developing an idea that he was working on; often, he would get so involved in what he was saying that he would miss his intended train and leave only when he had got whatever it was off his chest, scuttling out of the door with a shouted request that we ring Marjorie and let her know which train he was now hoping to catch.

These sessions were tremendously enjoyable – Arthur was a very funny man – but for me they were the equivalent of a university course in economics (without the mathematics, of course, for which Arthur had little time). They were also an indication of his generosity of spirit: he cared, and he cared that we cared. But even these interactions with Arthur were not enough to make my working day consistently interesting, and after two years or so I was bored and frustrated, and on the point of resigning in search of a more rewarding job. Arthur saw that the advent of our journal, *Economic Affairs*, in 1980 would not only serve its principal purpose of deploying market analysis over a far wider spread of subjects than the Hobart Papers and other IEA publications could address; it might also persuade me to remain at the Institute. Although he never mentioned it himself, I later learned that he had insisted both on a diminution of my administrative tasks so that I could formally become his assistant, and on a pay rise – a minor one, of course: we used to joke sourly at the IEA that Ralph measured our loyalty to the cause by the extent to which he could depress our salaries. It was now that my seven years of closest cooperation with Arthur began – as enriching an experience as I have known.

Economic Affairs: punchy and punctual

Economic Affairs was initially quarterly, and a journal; we decided that it was neither covering enough material nor reaching a big enough audience, and so Arthur managed to persuade the trustees that from 1985 onwards it should be bimonthly and a magazine. But our editorial approach was the same: at conferences, in conversations, at the Hobart Lunches, which took place at the IEA on the last Friday of every month and attracted thirty to forty academics, businessmen, politicians and other moulders of opinion, young and old, we would be on the lookout for unusual and interesting ideas that might form the basis of articles in *Economic Affairs* – five or six major articles and a handful of shorter commentaries. For Arthur one of the advantages of the journal over the other IEA publications was that it gave him a platform for more immediate comment on the issues of the day – and he could be a good deal more provocative there, too, than in the closely argued analysis of the main IEA output.

In July 1982, for example, when the Thatcher government was anxiously watching the unemployment figures mount towards the 3 million mark and the press was beginning to wonder whether the social fabric of the country would bear the strain, Arthur saw the opportunity of striking a blow for truth and wrote an editorial[5] which argued that the fact of 3 million unemployed was neither here nor there; what mattered was the length of time for which each individual was unemployed: with an efficient labour market that allowed people to find new jobs swiftly, it wouldn't matter if twice the current number of people were jobless – indeed, if there were rapid reinsertion into the labour force, a figure of 6 million unemployed might be the sign of a healthy economy. Arthur's editorial had the explosive force – to quote a memorable phrase of Dave Barry's – of throwing a squirrel into a roomful of Labrador retrievers. The press went over the top, encouraged, perhaps, by our press releases underlining Arthur's arbitrary total: 'Economist calls for six million unemployed' leapt from headline after headline the next Monday morning. Arthur's argument had reached millions – and taken mention of *Economic Affairs*, then still in its early days, with it.

Another incendiary idea that Arthur managed to prime for maximum press attention came in the form of an article from Richard Stapleton, then Professor of Business Finance at the Manchester Business School. Dick argued[6] that the relative efficiency of the German and Japanese economies, and the sclerosis of the British, could be attributed to the outcome of World War II: in Germany and Japan defeat had broken the grips of the interest groups that in victorious Britain had been able to maintain their privileged positions unbowed. Our press release naughtily suggested that Britain had been the real loser, and the journalists took the bait; once again the argument and its forum reached an audience of millions.

Working on *Economic Affairs*

Each issue of *Economic Affairs* involved Arthur and me, and Ruth Croxford, our long-suffering but highly efficient secretary, in regular meetings to ensure a lively publication and a wide spread of topics – which again we used to maximise attention. As each issue reached publication, I would dictate a series of press releases, vetted by Arthur, giving the essence of each of the major articles (sometimes ten or twelve press releases per issue), sending a copy to the specialist correspondents of all of the main newspapers – labour, education, agriculture, etc. When we were lucky, several of them would file a story on his specialist subject, not knowing that elsewhere in the building his colleagues were doing the same. This approach worked spectacularly on one occasion when the news editor of the *Financial Times*, faced with a phalanx of articles, obviously decided that resistance was futile and published four of them side by side in a huge mosaic filling the top half of one of the home-news pages.

Our editorial procedures evolved slowly over the years we worked together. We commissioned articles as we encountered the ideas, referring the news to each other for approval (an unnecessary courtesy on Arthur's part, of course, but typical of his thoughtfulness). To begin with, Arthur would work on a copy of each text, covering the page with markings and filling the margins with comments and questions for the author. Since his handwriting was often difficult to decipher (not least because of the disease, contracted during World War II, which affected his joints – see Chapter 1) and his comments were frequently more forthright than diplomacy preferred, I would then, in those pre-computer days, take a bottle of Tippex and prepare a clean version for the author, rephrasing Arthur's questions a shade less combatively, and clearing out redundant text. Many of his more forthright comments were obviously intended for me, rather than the author; I realise with hindsight that he was training me, helping me understand the insights of his craft, and with time he left more and more of the subediting to me, contenting himself with making sure that the analysis held water. But he read and commented on everything; even when in 1987 I took over as editor, releasing Arthur to spend more time on his own writing, I made sure that he saw everything that went into the publication – and on a couple of occasions, when editorials expressing my more overtly libertarian sympathies ruffled conservative feathers in the office, Arthur nobly stepped forward to say that I had his full sanction.

Concern for clarity

Arthur's concern in everything he wrote or edited was clarity. Any editor worth the condiment, of course, is on the lookout for sloppy writing; Arthur's objection to loose language was further informed by his classical liberalism. So he would object to a word like 'level', not only because it obscured a more precise meaning; it also misrepresented the subject at hand, as in a phrase like 'price level', which suggested some fictitious macroeconomic aggregate. 'Water has a level,' he would say; 'prices don't.' 'Level' as a quantifier was outlawed, too, to be replaced by more precise words, such as 'degree' or 'volume'. Government 'levels' became 'strata' or 'tiers'. 'Need' meaning merely 'require' was out: a 'need' in Arthur's hands really was a necessity – warmth, food, shelter, emotion. 'Just' meaning 'only' earned a contemptuous crossing-through since a text that overused it would lose force if the word were then required to mean 'equitable'. 'While' would disappear, guilty of causing confusion: if someone was doing A while someone else was doing B, did it indicate contemporaneity or contrast?

Some of his knee-jerk editorial reactions were provoked more by his general humanist instincts than because they signalled careless analysis. The word 'great' was guaranteed to generate a gouge on the manuscript when one of our authors used it simply to express intensity: 'great poverty', 'great distress'. Arthur's objection was twofold: there was no point in dignifying suffering; and he liked to keep his powder dry, so that, if he were to describe, say, Hayek as 'a great thinker', the encomium would retain its impact. Arthur took care that in his hands words meant exactly what they should.

It wasn't simply a question of style, of course. His aim was always to act as his author's most sceptical reader: he would hone an argument, poke its weak spots, raise objections his writers hadn't thought of, so that by the time it reached print, the case was as well made as it might be. In *Economic Affairs*, of course, where the larger articles were 2,000–3,000 words long and the shorter commentaries and other pieces around the 1,000-word mark, he didn't have the scope for the forensic examination of an argument required in his work on the Hobart Papers and other IEA publications, but his editorial intervention was no less rigorous.

On one occasion we thought we had found a light-hearted way of letting our authors see the kind of writing we were hoping to receive. I had dropped off an edited version of a book review to its author, Brian Micklethwait, then as now a stalwart of the Libertarian Alliance. Brian took one look at the butchering his text had received and blurted out in amused umbrage: 'Bloody hell, you lot would edit Shakespeare!' When I reported the reaction to Arthur, he laughed as loudly as I had – and then immediately saw that the idea could be put to good use. We asked Brian to edit Hamlet's soliloquy in the manner he might expect from us; I then tightened the text a little more and marked it up as I would a draft being returned to one of our writers, and we reproduced it photographically in the journal. We received numerous notes of amused appreciation – but not one of our authors seemed to realise that the exercise had a didactic purpose.

A feature of Arthur's own writings which also informed his

editing was his insistence on treating his ideological adversaries with courtesy, no matter how profoundly he disagreed with them. He was excited enough by a phrase in a letter from Hayek while we were working on an article of his on socialist calculation[7] to suggest he hadn't come across it before: *Suaviter in modo, fortiter in re* – roughly translated, 'Gently in your manner, firmly on your facts'. Just as IEA papers sought the views of opponents to their central argument (and still do), we exposed articles to criticism in a feature called 'Two Views'. For this Arthur had occasion to commission writers whose reasoning he held in disdain – but he handled their texts with the same considerate attention to detail as he did those of his close friends and associates.

In all his editorial activities Arthur seemed to hold to heart what is probably the most important phrase in all economics: Adam Smith's statement, in Book Two of *The Wealth of Nations*, that 'Consumption is the sole end and purpose of all production'. As editors, we must be the servants of the reader. So anything that left the reader to struggle with an argument would not only have been a dereliction of his professional duty as an editor: it also ran counter to his most deeply held beliefs as economist and political philosopher. On the same grounds, imperatives that exhorted the reader to 'note', 'recall', 'observe', and so on, were out: it was no place of ours, as respectful producers, to order our consumers about. Arthur's mind and his method were all of a piece.

Among young and old

Another of the attractions of *Economic Affairs* for Arthur was that it allowed him to encourage younger writers, whose experience or abilities might not justify a full-length IEA paper but who had something interesting to say. It may be a truism to say so, but Arthur had boundless faith in the young. He encouraged promising students and young graduates to attend the Hobart Lunches, and when he and Marjorie held their open days at the Thatched

Cottage at Godden Green, outside Sevenoaks, there were always young faces among the more distinguished countenances.

His encouragement went beyond professional helpfulness and the parental solicitude that he and Marjorie showed to so many of us, earning our enduring affection, even love from those of us fortunate to grow close to them. After he and Marjorie had founded Economic and Literary Books in 1985 to publish *Poppies and Roses: A Story of Courage*, Marjorie's memoir of her war-hero father, Arthur commissioned twenty of us to contribute an essay to a volume he called *The 'New Right' Enlightenment*, to which he added a double subtitle: 'The Spectre that Haunts the Left: Essays by Young Writers'. Some of these 'young writers' were already established figures in their thirties, but others were students barely out of school. And not all of them were convinced liberals: one or two were unashamedly of a collectivist cast of mind, but it was enough for Arthur that they were prepared to consider the market as a means of allocating scarce goods and services for him to find room for their sceptical views. We worked together on the texts, and I recall Arthur's concern, as in *Economic Affairs*, that his charges express their arguments as clearly as possible, even when he disagreed with them.

I can't have been the only one of those twenty writers who Arthur's invitation had forced to articulate his or her thoughts in as concise and as coherent an expression as we had yet attempted. I mentioned that Arthur was one of the two most influential figures in my life. The other was Hans Keller, the Hampstead-based musician and writer born in Vienna in 1919, and a Jewish refugee from oppression in 1938, as Arthur's parents had been a generation and more earlier. Having managed to crystallise my outlook on life in an essay called 'In defence of chaos' in *The 'New Right' Enlightenment*, I was intending to present a copy to Hans, as a token of esteem and gratitude, and hoping that it would allow me to bring these two men together. But Hans died, a victim of motor neurone disease, on 6 November 1985, while the book was still in production, and so my chance of introducing him and Arthur to each other evaporated. It remains a bitter regret. Hans, too, was a passionate anti-collectivist (he once entitled an essay 'Thinkers of the world, disunite!'), and I am certain that he and Arthur would have taken prodigious pleasure in each other's company. Arthur enjoyed classical music, opera in particular, but his knowledge was that of the enlightened outsider; Hans, as perceptive a writer on music as there has been, was unfamiliar with the economic literature that buttressed the methodological individualism that he shared with Arthur – death obstructed a friendship both men would have found profoundly rewarding, and I offer their shades my apology that I didn't feel it was my place to bring them together earlier.

There is one thing I'm proud of, though. To mark Arthur's 70th birthday in May 1986 I commissioned, without his knowledge, essays from the most prestigious of the economists he had worked most closely with over the preceding decades: James Buchanan, Ronald Coase, Milton Friedman, Friedrich Hayek, W. H. Hutt, Israel Kirzner, Patrick Minford, Gordon Tullock, Alan Walters and Basil Yamey, publishing the resulting Festschrift under the title *The Unfinished Agenda*; Ralph Harris supplied a prologue and a subtitle: 'Essays on the political economy of government policy in honour of Arthur Seldon'. Somehow we managed to see the book through production without Arthur discovering what was afoot; I even succeeded in taking a series of photographs of him for the front and back covers without raising suspicion. He did mention later that the absence of discussion of any publication for May during the Institute's planning meetings indicated that something was afoot, but he knew no more than that. At the end of the dinner organised at the IEA to mark the birthday itself, I asked for silence and, reaching behind the various IEA papers ranged along the mantelpiece, pulled out a leather-bound copy of the book and presented it to Arthur. It remains the only time I ever saw him lost for words.

PART IV

ARTHUR SELDON'S INTELLECTUAL CONTRIBUTION

9

An overview

Arthur Seldon's distinctive contribution to classical liberal thought in the twentieth century came through his own writings, through his editorial work at the Institute of Economic Affairs and through the influence he had on others.[1]

Seldon had few hobbies, though he was interested in cricket (see Chapter 7) and in opera. He immersed himself in economic ideas and his interests in those ideas were very wide, as demonstrated by his decision, after much thought, to undertake the monumental task of compiling a dictionary of economics. The first edition in 1965 of *Everyman's Dictionary of Economics* was produced in collaboration with his friend Fred Pennance, but the much-revised edition of 1975 is almost entirely the work of Seldon.[2] The dictionary, which is Volume 3 in *The Collected Works*, runs to over seven hundred pages. It is unusual among dictionaries of economics in two important respects. First, it gives a prominent place to the history of economic ideas (about one eighth of the total entries), which is consistent with Seldon's view that economists should acknowledge their debt to their predecessors and build on their work, as he always did. The dictionary gives concise biographies of the leading classical economists and of some of the most famous twentieth-century economists. It also describes some of the leading schools of economic thought, such as the Austrian, Cambridge, Chicago,

Manchester and Virginia schools. Second, as well as setting out mainstream economic views (with which Seldon was well acquainted), the dictionary explains the classical liberal perspective. To take one example,[3] the entry for 'Competition', after describing the various market forms used by neoclassical economists (perfect competition, imperfect competition, monopoly, etc.), goes on to say that the most relevant concept of competition is the Hayekian process of discovery.

> Competition in its fundamental social, dynamic purpose is a device for *discovering* demand and supply (in their everyday sense, i.e. what people want and how to give it to them) rather than merely *responding* to existing wants and techniques. [Italics in original][4]

The dictionary, though now inevitably somewhat dated in terms of events, is still a worthwhile part of any economist's library, giving as it does a clear sense of how economic thought has evolved over the centuries, and setting out not only mainstream economic ideas but the challenge to those ideas from the great classical liberal scholars.[5]

Seldon's own broad view of economics encompassed both mainstream and classical ideas. He described his thinking as based on 'the teaching at the LSE in the mid 1930s' and deriving fundamentally from Adam Smith's ideas – that 'individual men and women best escape from poverty and inadequacy by exchanging in free markets the products of the skills they acquired by concentrating on their individual faculties'.[6] But he was not a theorist, in the sense of making original contributions to economic theory as, for instance, did Friedrich Hayek and Milton Friedman. Nor was he, except in the early post-war years, a hands-on applied economist, who used the methods and techniques of others to deal with practical problems. His contribution was firmly in the field of ideas, but he was essentially a synthesiser who used, as a base for all he did, the work of the classical liberal economists which he had absorbed at the LSE, and then integrated within that body of thought newer ideas such as public choice, monetarist economics and neo-Austrian economics to produce a synthesis appropriate for practical policy in the age in which he lived. That synthesis, which, with Ralph Harris, he publicised so effectively, is a very powerful body of ideas which allowed him to demonstrate – for example, in works like *Capitalism* – that the capitalist system maximises freedom and is flexible and adaptive, standing in contrast to the inflexible and totalitarian nature of socialism. In one of Seldon's most notable phrases, he summarised the contrast as between corrigible capitalism and incorrigible socialism.[7]

Although it took Seldon most of his lifetime to arrive at the synthesis, which is most clearly displayed in the very wide-ranging *Capitalism*, there is a consistency in his work in that, from his earliest writings as a recent graduate,[8] his work is firmly in the classical liberal tradition. From the beginning, there is an emphasis, harking back to Adam Smith but standing in contrast to the economic orthodoxy of the early post-war years, on the advantages that flow from relying on markets in which consumers choose freely among competing suppliers. The synthesis that Seldon achieved in his own mind is not just an important feature of his own writings. Its wider significance is that it infused and held together the work of the Institute of Economic Affairs as expressed in the writings of many authors. Because of Seldon's influence, out of the disparate subjects about which IEA authors wrote came a consistent message about the virtues of voluntary action and the dangers of government intervention. It was this message which was eventually so powerful in persuading public opinion and hence in engaging politicians who were anxious to catch the mood of the electorate.

At the centre of the Seldon synthesis is the process of competitive rivalry that gives freedom of choice to consumers and provides them with the 'power of exit' – that is, the ability to move away from suppliers they do not like. Classical economics, as developed by Adam Smith and his successors, had such ideas at its heart but the neoclassical economics that dominated microeconomic theory for the first three-quarters of the twentieth century moved away from such ideas towards formalised models which, implicitly or explicitly, regard the long-run equilibrium of 'perfect competition' as an ideal outcome. These models consider situations of equilibrium after competition has been exhausted and neglect the competitive process itself.[9] Classical ideas remained alive mainly in the writings of 'Austrian' economists such as Ludwig von Mises and later Friedrich Hayek, who generally rejected formalised equilibrium models and regarded competition, in Hayek's famous words, as a 'process of discovery' in which entrepreneurs find new ways of doing things.[10]

Hayek, who was instrumental in the founding of the IEA,[11] was a particularly important figure in the development of the Seldon synthesis. Seldon recognised the significance of Hayek's ideas, helped Hayek express his views in a form that made them more accessible (as Hayek acknowledged[12]) and expanded on them to shed new light on the nature of the capitalist system. That system, in Seldon's view, is founded on the Hayekian discovery process in which entrepreneurs are constantly seeking and exploiting new opportunities, which gives it an inherent flexibility and adaptability to change that does not exist in any other form of economic organisation so far known. Capitalism will adjust to changing preferences of consumers and it will absorb bigger shocks with little need for government intervention. Indeed, such intervention, in Seldon's view, tends to hinder the discovery process by curbing entrepreneurship – for instance, by taxes, subsidies and regulations that penalise the enterprising or by 'competition policies' that place barriers in the way of takeovers.

There may be certain goods and services that are 'public' in the sense that they will not be supplied in the 'right' quantity or not supplied at all under capitalism, but they are few and far between. A large proportion of the goods and services supplied by government are not 'public' at all, in Seldon's view. Government has encroached on the private sector, which otherwise would have supplied them. The welfare state was a mistake and is unsustainable. Education, health, pension provision can perfectly well be supplied privately, and their private supply would ensure both that suppliers responded to consumers' demands and that they were produced efficiently. At times, Seldon argues for a massive reduction in the share of the state in national product – down from over 40 per cent to 20 per cent or even 10 per cent – so that the state would come closer to being a supplier only of goods that would not be supplied privately.

Also incorporated in the Seldon synthesis are the conclusions of the public choice theorists who, starting in the United States in the 1950s, built on the work of Adam Smith and David Hume. Seldon was early to recognise the importance of their work, which was based on the view that people are much the same whether they work in the private or the 'public' sector, and that assuming that 'public servants' simply pursue the 'public interest' is unlikely to lead to useful predictions of their behaviour. Seldon realised that public choice theory, or the 'economics of politics', as it was often called in Britain, undermined the general case for government action based on 'market imperfection' and 'market failure' grounds. Governments were complex organisations, made up of individuals pursuing individual and organisational interests, so that it was far from clear that, even if the 'public interest' could be identified in a particular case, a government would be willing to pursue it. This view called into question the whole rationale of government intervention in the economy and, in effect, raised an anti-monopoly case against government action. A government in office can coerce and has a monopoly of policymaking. It is constrained only by infrequent elections. It has a much more powerful position than any private monopoly and, in general, there seems no reason to expect that its actions will enhance the welfare of the community.

One of the conclusions that Seldon drew from public choice theory and which caused him great concern was that there are very powerful self-interest forces in government that tend to promote expansion. These forces are so strong that they should be resisted, Seldon said, even to the extent of 'taking a risk on under-government'.[13] Both the Austrian and the public choice strands of the synthesis thus propel Seldon into mounting powerful arguments against government intervention.

To understand further the intellectual framework that Arthur Seldon developed, his work is discussed in the next three chapters under three headings – the virtues of capitalism, the problem of over-government and the perils of the welfare state. In each of these fields he made substantial contributions to economic ideas. In the first two he had a significant influence on policy by identifying the advantages of capitalism over socialism, by demonstrating the dangers of government intervention and by explaining his ideas so clearly that any intelligent person could understand them. He had less success with his ideas for reforming the welfare state, powerful though those ideas were, because of what he regarded as the timidity of politicians. But his influence may yet be felt since governments are still struggling with the problems he identified.

Concentrating on these three fields is not meant to imply that his contributions were limited to them. In his capacity as Editorial Director of the IEA, his influence was very wide. For example, it could be argued that Seldon contributed substantially to the development of monetary economics by recognising and publicising the work of Milton Friedman, Alan Walters, Patrick Minford and others who revived the monetary tradition in economics and thereby made a significant step forward in controlling inflation.[14] Similarly, through his publishing programme, he made a major contribution to the reform of labour laws in Britain and the reduction in trade union power, which were very important factors in Britain's economic revival. Indeed, in his role as Editorial Director, Seldon was instrumental in moving forward many areas of economics. But much of his own writing fits within the three broad subject areas discussed in the chapters that follow.

10

The virtues of capitalism

As Arthur Seldon's career advanced, his appreciation of capitalism as an economic system grew. His wide reading, his careful editing of the work of others, his own experiences of life and the constant debate in which he engaged confirmed the view that can be discerned even in his earliest writings that capitalism is a form of economic organisation that is superior to its competitors, particularly to socialism. Capitalism embodies incentives to which people naturally respond, it promotes efficiency, it adapts to change. Seldon recognised, of course, that not everyone is a winner under capitalism: some people may be disadvantaged but, in Seldon's view, it is not difficult to deal with such cases. Socialism, on the other hand, works against the grain of human nature, it does not promote efficiency, it results in rigidities that make adaptation to change hard. Moreover, capitalism maximises individual freedom, whereas socialism invariably leads to oppressive governments.

Seldon was concerned that the virtues of capitalism were not widely recognised. So he set about a task that not many economists in modern times have been willing to undertake – to explore the fundamental features of a capitalist economy and to contrast it with socialism. In considering Seldon's efforts, we should remember that for much of his working life, socialism had seemed to be in the ascendant. In the post-World War II years up to the 1980s, many intellectuals believed that communism, as practised in the Soviet Union and its satellites, was an efficient system of economic organisation, producing rapid economic growth, and that social democracy with significant government intervention was the way forward for Western societies. Such beliefs began to be shaken in the 1980s, partly because of the work of Seldon and his colleagues, but it was not until the 1990s, with the demise of communism throughout much of the world, the privatisation movement and the decline of interventionism in social democratic countries, that socialism seemed to be clearly on the way out. Seldon's main works about capitalism predated the fall of socialism: he was writing in the 1980s when the fate of socialism was much less clear than it appeared in the early years of the 21st century.

His wide-ranging book *Capitalism* is generally regarded as his finest achievement and is certainly one of the great contributions to the literature of classical liberalism of recent times. The view Seldon takes of capitalism is essentially 'Austrian', in the sense that a Hayekian process of competitive discovery lies at the centre of the system, and it incorporates the conclusions of the public choice school (discussed in more detail in the next chapter) and all Seldon's long-accumulated experience of learning about how markets and governments work. *Capitalism* summarises all that Seldon had learned about economics and the conclusions he had reached about the respective roles of voluntary action and state action.

Corrigible Capitalism, Incorrigible Socialism

Capitalism had its precursors. Seldon first set out the principal differences between capitalism and socialism in an IEA paper published in 1980, which grew out of a piece written in the same year for the New Zealand Employers' Federation entitled *A Credo for Private Enterprise*. These views were then amplified in his much longer *Capitalism*. His brief 1980 IEA paper was given one of his most inspired titles, *Corrigible Capitalism, Incorrigible Socialism*, which neatly summarises the main elements in his case. Capitalism is a dynamic, adaptive system, capable of dealing with its own faults: socialism is incapable of adaptation to changing circumstances, nor can it cope with its own internal problems. The defects of capitalism are remediable, whereas socialism is an irredeemable system. Seldon concludes his analysis of the two systems by arguing that government should withdraw from many of the activities it is pursuing, confining itself to the provision of genuine 'public goods' (which would not otherwise be supplied).

Given Seldon's views about the virtues of capitalism, he was puzzled that so many intellectuals were critical of a regime that was so beneficial to them as well as to others, and why there was such support for socialism. As he puts it, 'Private enterprise has produced the wealth of the world, yet it has suffered more calumny and obloquy than any other system. Its alternative, state economy, has retarded the production of wealth; yet it has been lauded and deified.'[1]

In *Corrigible Capitalism* Seldon attempted to correct this view, which he found so misleading. The first part of the paper considers four supposed defects of capitalism. First, there is the idea that capitalism produces **'inequality'** – more accurately described by Seldon as differences in incomes. These differences, says Seldon, are consequences not of capitalism but of the unequal distribution of talents. They can be remedied within the capitalist system by means such as a reverse income tax and vouchers that give extra spending power to the poor.

Monopoly is the second 'defect' addressed by Seldon. As he points out, the capitalist system has its own inbuilt remedy for monopoly: where monopoly profits are being earned, competitors will enter markets and compete away any 'excess'. Only in cases where there are government-erected barriers to entry – such as state monopolies – will the capitalist remedy not work. Government monopolies are a much more serious problem than temporary monopolies under capitalism.

Worker alienation under capitalism is another supposed

defect. Seldon argues, however, that 'industrial democracy', with worker participation in management decisions, is not the answer. Under capitalism, companies can prosper only by supplying what consumers want. Consumers are thus empowered under capitalism, as they are not under socialism. Moreover, under capitalism (unlike socialism) employees can own shares in their firms.

The presence of **'external' costs and benefits**, which are not taken into account by firms in their decision-making, is another favourite target of critics of capitalism. Seldon asks why this 'defect' is attributed to capitalism. In the case of environmental pollution, for example, 'Collectivist smoke pollutes social democratic Sweden and Austria, or communist Poland and Bulgaria, as much as market smoke pollutes Britain, Canada and Australia' (p. 24).

The problem arises where property rights are not properly defined. Unlike socialist systems, capitalism can define and enforce these rights.

Having dealt with these remediable defects of capitalism, Seldon moves on to the 'incurable defects' of state enterprise, considering not only authoritarian societies but also 'social democracy', which is 'paternalist in spirit and benign in execution' (p. 27).

Ignorance is the most basic problem of any form of state planning. 'Without markets, state economy is blind' (p. 30) because there is no parallel in state systems to the market process in which suppliers discover the preferences of consumers and supply them.

Inefficiency is another fundamental defect of state action. Because of the ignorance problem, shortages and surpluses, compared with what consumers want, are the norm.

Social conflict is also a common characteristic of a state regime because minority views are inevitably disregarded.

Monopoly is inherent in state action, says Seldon. A state economy 'lives by monopoly and abhors competition' (p. 33). In the absence of competitive markets, the market discovery mechanism does not operate.

Coercion is also inherent and the greater the degree of state control, the more citizens are coerced.

Corruption is a feature of state regimes. Markets go underground and the heavy taxes that are required to finance state activity tend to be avoided or evaded. Politicians become creators of favours and officials turn into dispensers of contracts.

Finally, in Seldon's list, is the issue of **secrecy**. He points to the concealment of information in the Soviet Union, which was still in existence when he wrote. Social democracy may seem more benign but under social democracy there is always pressure for more state control and so it also has a problem of secrecy.

Seldon concludes his analysis of the strengths of capitalism and the failings of socialism by saying that, whatever the faults of markets, government failure is the more serious problem because its faults are incurable within the regime. Not surprisingly, he takes a classical liberal view of government. Its activities should be confined to laying down a general framework of law rather than detailed rules, and to the supply of goods and services that are genuinely 'public' and which must therefore be financed from general taxation. Although at the time he wrote the failings of socialism in practice were not so apparent as they are now, Seldon was optimistic about the power of markets to overcome political forces. In his paper, he makes an interesting (and accurate) prediction: with the British Labour Party dividing into socialist and social democratic components, it would never rule again. In a letter to *The Times* of London a month after *Corrigible Capitalism* was published, Seldon expressed the point very precisely and correctly – 'Labour as we know it will never rule again'.[2]

Capitalism

In *Capitalism*, published by Blackwell in 1990 and written between October 1988 and October 1989 after Seldon had retired from active involvement in the IEA, he returns to the analysis of capitalist systems.[3] The essential issues treated in this long book (over four hundred pages, compared with fifty for *Corrigible Capitalism*) are, of course, the same, but Seldon produces much more evidence and more detailed and refined arguments in his attempt to convert the critics of capitalism. As in the earlier paper, Seldon is not a defender of capitalism so much as an enthusiastic supporter. His preface makes clear that capitalism 'requires not defence but celebration'.

The arguments he sets out are clear and compelling. The synthesis of the case for capitalism that Seldon produces is based on ideas that he had been considering for about fifty years since their foundations were established at the LSE in the 1930s. Those ideas had been supplemented and reinforced by the insights of 'Austrian' economists such as Friedrich Hayek and the public choice school (see Chapter 11 below), by the writings of other economists in the hundreds of IEA papers that Seldon had commissioned and edited, by the controversies in which Seldon had engaged, and by his observation of the dire state into which the British economy fell in the 1970s and the growing problems of the communist world.

In the ten years that had elapsed since the publication of *Corrigible Capitalism*, the world had begun to move away from socialism so that Seldon was less isolated in his views, which would, in 1980, have seemed extreme to the vast majority of intellectual opinion. Indeed, some of the predictions he had made in the earlier paper about the future of socialism now looked much more plausible. He was writing *Capitalism* at the time of glasnost and perestroika in the Soviet Union, and it was becoming clearer that the communist experiment was on the brink of collapse. In *Capitalism*, Seldon generalises his predictions about socialism, concluding that the 'political life of socialism' is likely to end in the 1990s (p. 83).

Seldon's preface explains the central theme of the book. He is doubtful about 'political democracy' as a guarantor of freedom: the market is more certain. For capitalism to 'yield its best results … the political process must be confined to the minimal duties of the state'. The anti-capitalist views of intellectuals, about which he had expressed puzzlement in *Corrigible Capitalism*, he explains by identifying a tendency to contrast capitalism as it is, with its flaws exposed and often exaggerated, with an idealised vision of a socialist society that in practice could never exist. This idealised version of socialism, Seldon argues, is deeply entrenched in the educational system in Britain and other 'mixed' economies. He recalls that he came up against the system himself when at school. As Seldon explains in Chapter 2 of *Capitalism*, he was fortunate to be taught in the sixth form by a history master who introduced him to classical liberal ideas, of whose existence he had previously been unaware. Seldon goes on to say that his doubts about socialism were 'powerfully confirmed at the LSE' (p. 94) and by the lessons of 'war socialism'.

One of the arguments deployed by socialist thinkers, which still lingered at the time *Capitalism* was being written, was that resistance to the spread of socialism was pointless because socialism was inevitable. Seldon tackles the 'inevitability of socialism' argument head-on in Chapter 3. Socialism was being abandoned by left-wing politicians, he argues, because it had been seen to have failed in practice. It is capitalism that, as a superior economic system, is inevitable.

On the theme of socialism in practice, in Chapter 4 Seldon analyses socialism in the Soviet Union, presciently commenting that it is a 'political interlude'. Capitalism will return to Russia because it has been shown in the Soviet Union that the 'expectations of the masses' cannot be satisfied given the political centralisation that socialism requires. In another far-sighted prediction, Seldon says that China will have to go capitalist in the 1990s in order to meet the demands of the masses and allow living standards to rise.

Seldon was, in much of his work, concerned about the view that political democracy is sufficient to guarantee freedom. This form of democracy relies on headcounting and tends to override the wishes of minorities, unlike the market, which, following Lionel Robbins, Seldon regards as an instrument of democracy since it amounts to a continuous referendum on the goods and services on offer to consumers. Seldon stresses the 'power of exit' through the market, which allows consumers to escape from suppliers they do not favour, and which he argues in Chapter 4 is always more effective than the power of 'voice', which is the right to participate in political action. Capitalism and political democracy are compatible and reinforce each other; socialism is not compatible with political democracy because it relies on centralised planning and coercion.

Central to Seldon's views about the market is the advantage of reliance on the price system, which is the 'device for deciding where resources are to be used according to individual preferences' (p. 196). Market pricing cannot be combined with government ownership because there is no way of knowing what costs and prices would emerge in a competitive market unless such a market exists. 'Political pricing' is the likely outcome of centralisation. In Chapters 5 and 6 Seldon emphasises the benefits of allocation by price. Socialism does not promote equality of access to resources, as is sometimes claimed, he says. Allocation by means other than price means that the articulate middle classes do best.

In Chapters 7 and 8, Seldon lists ten recent developments that he believes strengthen the case for capitalism. They are worth mentioning because they show how Seldon constantly monitored the economics literature and brought new developments into his synthesis of the case for capitalism. The ten are: rejection of the Marxist interpretation of history; the renewed emphasis of economic historians on the role of property rights in economic growth; the move away from macroeconomics towards microeconomics and the study of market processes; the growth of the public choice school (see Chapter 11 of this book); a more realistic view of government regulation which recognises that regulators are often captured or at least heavily influenced by those they are supposed to regulate; realisation that most of the goods and services supplied by government are not genuine 'public goods' that the private sector would not supply;

awareness that the case for intervention to deal with externalities is often exploited for political reasons; an improved understanding of the role of money in the economy and the need for
politicians to stand back from macroeconomic control; invasion
by economists of areas of research (such as marriage, the family
and crime) previously dominated by sociologists and political
scientists; and a reaction against the 'fiction' of the social welfare
function which would aggregate individual preferences to create
a supposedly representative choice that could be imposed by
central planners.

Seldon devotes Chapter 9 to a discussion of some criticisms
of capitalism. He rejects the 'contradictions of capitalism' argument of the Marxists, the democratic socialist critique that, in
effect, compares imperfect markets with perfect political processes, and the criticisms of political conservatives in Britain who
are wary of markets.

In Chapter 10, Seldon sketches a 'vision of capitalism' in
which the political process is 'confined to the minimum of una-
voidably collective functions' (p. 288) and can accommodate free
markets. He refers favourably to Adam Smith's view that government should do only what cannot be done by the market.
Capitalism, however, says Seldon, has never had such a government. In Britain, government has taken over functions that were
being performed well by the private sector. He produces evidence in Chapter 11 to show that education, health, housing and
pensions were developing well in the nineteenth century before
the government intervened, jumping on a 'galloping horse' and
slowing it down (p. 337).

Does capitalism lack a moral base, as is the charge? Not so,
argues Seldon, and, following Adam Smith, he produces a very
explicit statement in Chapter 12 of why the pursuit of self-interest in competitive markets leads to desirable results. The service
of self is universal and capitalism provides the necessary incentives to harness self-service. 'The virtue of capitalism is that it …
does not require good men and women. The vice of socialism is
that men and women who may start with good intentions, but

who are skilled in acquiring coercive power, can use it to do harm' (p. 344). The corrigibility of capitalism comes in again here – 'The market discovers and ejects its bad people sooner than politics' (p. 345).

Chapter 13, 'The verdict', summarises Seldon's views about the superiority of capitalism over other known systems of economic organisation. It is the most effective means of organising human cooperation. Unlike other systems, it combines high productivity with individual liberty. And it is conducive to peace because the internationalisation of markets produces a vested interest in peace.

The final chapter of *Capitalism* again demonstrates Seldon's optimism about its future. Marxism is on the wane; 'obstructive interests' are in decline; prominent individuals have appeared, such as Margaret Thatcher and Ronald Reagan, who have put their faith in capitalism; and there are 'conspiring circumstances', such as the growth of underground economies, that are allowing people to escape from governments and particularly from socialism. Markets will triumph over political forces because people are behind them.

11

The problem of over-government

Another major element in Arthur Seldon's intellectual framework is the economic analysis of government, exemplified in the last few decades by the American 'public choice' school (often referred to in Britain as the 'economics of politics'). Seldon, as a classical liberal scholar, had from his LSE days onwards been suspicious of government intervention in markets. Following in the tradition of Adam Smith and other classical economists, he doubted the claims that government action would necessarily be welfare-improving and he favoured reliance on voluntary action through markets.

In the twentieth century, however, the move away from classical economics had led to the near-loss of scepticism about the benefits of government action. Neoclassical economics emphasised the 'imperfections' and 'failures' of markets and relied on government action to deal with these supposed problems. The nature of government itself was little analysed by economists. It was a 'black box' whose contents were not examined. It was represented, explicitly or implicitly, as an omniscient and altruistic body that could always be brought into a market to put matters to rights. These simplifying (indeed simplistic) assumptions allowed economists to carry out formal analysis of markets, generally to compare them to the perfectly competitive ideal, and when they found 'imperfections' and 'failures' (as they invariably did) to recommend various forms of action by a perfect interventionist.

Although Seldon and other classical liberal thinkers were well aware of government as it was – rather than as it was portrayed in neoclassical economic analysis – it was not until economists began the formal analysis of government that it became clear how misleading were the predictions yielded by neoclassical assumptions. The development of the public choice school in the United States was crucial in bringing about this change of view.

Public choice has its roots in the work of classical economists such as Adam Smith and David Hume[1] but modern work in this field dates back only about fifty years. A major breakthrough occurred when, in 1957, Anthony Downs, an American economist, published *An Economic Theory of Democracy*,[2] which applied standard economic analysis to political processes.[3] According to Downs, political life is analogous to economic life. There is a political marketplace in which exchanges take place, as they do in other marketplaces. In particular, policies are exchanged for votes. Instead of politicians trying to get into power in order to pursue policies (the standard view of the 'public-spirited' politician), they put forward policies in order to get into power. In other words, they set out what they propose to do in an effort to attract votes. Citizens have little incentive to find out what politicians are actually likely to do if they attain office: gathering such information would be time-consuming and it might be misleading anyway, as the politicians might not carry out their promises. Against these costs of information-gathering must be set the likely benefits of voting, which are extremely small since the individual's effect on the election result is infinitesimal. Hence the 'rationality of ignorance'. Except for a small number of political enthusiasts, spending time collecting information about the likely actions of politicians is simply not worthwhile.

Parties respond by producing minimal amounts of

information, often in the form of slogans designed to attract votes, which can readily be absorbed by the electorate. The political process in a two-party representative system, as in the United States or Britain, is thus similar to a duopoly in economic theory in which two interdependent firms compete, often in terms of advertising and minor product differentiation. Downs's work was identified by Harry Johnson, one of the great economic theorists of the twentieth century, in his Inaugural Lecture at the LSE in 1967,[4] as one of the most important recent developments in economics, departing, as it did, from previous notions of 'government as the impartial servant of the public good … which leaves unexplained much of the actual activity and policy of government'.

The notion of a political marketplace brings economic theory to bear on political action and moves it away from the idealised view of government embodied in neoclassical economics. As public choice theory has developed in the last 50 years, it has produced many more ideas relevant to the analysis of government. For example, it has demonstrated that governments, which are always short of information, are often heavily influenced by pressure groups which appear to have such information. It has shown the inconsistency in neoclassical theory of treating individuals in government as public spirited, whereas individuals in the private sector are self-interested – what James Buchanan, one of the founders of public choice, has described as the 'bifurcated man' assumption. It has analysed the behaviour of bureaucrats, who are very influential in government. In general, it has made it much more difficult for economists to assume perfect government rather than, in their prescriptions, working out what a real-world government is likely to do.

The advent of public choice theory was very significant for Arthur Seldon and the IEA.[5] It opened up a whole new research programme, much of it carried out in the United States, which showed, by formal economic analysis, that reservations about the benefits of government action were justified. Seldon, who was always looking out for new developments in economics which reinforced the case for markets, seized on public choice analysis. He and Harris imported it into Britain in the mid-1970s, just as they had imported monetary economics – via a lecture by Milton Friedman – a few years earlier, in 1970.[6] In 1978, they organised a conference on 'The Economics of Politics', the proceedings of which were subsequently published as an IEA paper,[7] which was addressed by some of the leading figures in the field, including James Buchanan (who was awarded a Nobel Prize in 1986 for his work in public choice). Earlier Seldon had persuaded Gordon Tullock, one of the other founding fathers of public choice, to write a paper for the IEA in 1976. This paper, *The Vote Motive*, of course edited by Seldon, was very successful in opening the eyes of many people to the actual behaviour of governments. Tullock himself was enthusiastic about his IEA paper, and Seldon's editing, which made it accessible to a wide audience.[8] It was translated into at least a dozen languages, giving Tullock's views international exposure. In keeping with the IEA's mission, the book had a very practical purpose.

> … it was perhaps the first non-technical presentation of public choice analysis … directed more towards students, journalists and decision-makers than to the relatively narrow circles of economists, political scientists, legal scholars and sociologists already familiar with the approach.[9]

The public choice approach, from the time of the 1978 conference onwards, became an integral part of the thinking of Seldon and his colleagues and, through Seldon's influence, it was incorporated in IEA publications.[10]

As far as Seldon's own writing was concerned, he readily absorbed and used the conclusions of the public choice school. He quickly recognised that one of the implications is that there may well be a tendency towards over-government. Governments have the power to coerce, for example by taxing or imposing regulations, which leads them to go beyond their traditional functions (such as national defence, maintenance of law and order and the safeguarding of property rights). Even though governments plead the need to supply 'public' goods and services, Seldon argued on numerous occasions that there is little genuinely 'public' about most of their activity. No more than about one third of what the British government supplies could be justified as 'public'. The tendency to over-government is very damaging, according to Seldon, because government failure is rife: governments have insufficient knowledge to identify and achieve 'public interest' goals and, even if they could determine what is in the 'public interest', they lack the incentive to pursue it if it conflicts with their own goals.

Seldon's major works on over-government are in Volume 5 of *The Collected Works*. By the late 1970s, when he would have been aware of the work of the public choice school, a number of his papers stress the over-government issue. In 'Change by degree or by convulsion', written in 1978 as a contribution to a collection of papers published by the IEA on whether the open society would survive,[11] Seldon deals with the problem of union power, arguing that governments have brought this problem on themselves by encroaching on the private sector using false claims that they are providing 'public goods'. He was optimistic, nevertheless, on the grounds that economic laws will overcome political power – the British people will want to restore the market. Again in 'Individual liberty, public goods and representative government: lessons from the West and escape for the East', published in 1979,[12] Seldon returns to the over-government theme, stressing the dangers of majority rule and the threat from the special interests that influence government.

More substantial writings on the same theme came towards the end of Seldon's life. One of these was a book published by the IEA in 1998, *The Dilemma of Democracy*,[13] which he intended as a complement to *Capitalism*. In it, he brings together and expands on the criticisms of political democracy that are explicit or implicit in much of his earlier work, but particularly in

Capitalism. Democracy has failed, says Seldon, in the sense that nowhere has Lincoln's vision been fulfilled. Nowhere is there government of the people, by the people, for the people. Instead, majority rule has become 'the source of arbitrary rule. Political democracy represents some of the people more than the others' (p. 89). Seldon uses the work of the public choice theorists to explain the tendency to over-government. Members of governments pursue their own interests and are also unduly swayed by the activities of pressure groups that seek favours from government for their members. These groups thrive on the shortage of information that faces government and provide information themselves, knowing that lobbying is potentially a high-return activity.

As ever, Seldon is optimistic, despite the trend towards greater government. Following Böhm-Bawerk, he expects economic laws to overcome political power. Governments may seem powerful but they are not as powerful as market forces. Citizens are already using markets, including 'shadow' economies, to escape from government. Governments should, Seldon says, recognise that they should retreat before they are rolled back by people's choices. The state should halve its size from around 40 per cent to around 20 per cent of national income.

Seldon's last work of substance was published by the IEA in 2000. It was part of a set of Readings, written with Gordon Tullock and Gordon Brady, which explained the elements of the public choice approach. At Seldon's suggestion, it was entitled *Government: Whose Obedient Servant?*[14] In it, Seldon explains the problem of collective choice that dogs all government decisions. 'The indirect results that emerge in the politically-decided production of goods and services are usually very different from those that would be chosen directly by the public itself' (p. 150).

The existing 'democratic' system embodies a voting system that does not properly reflect voters' preferences, rent-seeking and log-rolling dominate decision-making, and the recommendations of bureaucrats reflect their own interests. Government is excessive and government-provided services are mediocre, with choice denied. He instances the welfare state, which he would like to see dismantled, permitting citizens to spend their own money on the goods and services they choose. As in *The Dilemma of Democracy*, he expects the problem of over-government to be corrected as people escape via markets. In the 21st century, people will find 'they can escape as they never could before' (p. 190).

In 2000 Seldon also published a short paper, 'On the liberal emancipation of mankind',[15] in which he returns to the over-government theme but goes beyond his earlier work in arguing that Böhm-Bawerk's question about the relative strengths of political power and economic law was answered in the 1990s. In his boldest prediction, Seldon says that in the first two decades of the 21st century the growing escape from government will reduce the share of government in national income to only 10 per cent, both in North America and Europe. The state is, he claims, in retreat because of the superiority of the market.

12

The perils of the welfare state

Many people associate Arthur Seldon particularly with his critique of state welfare, and it is indeed true that, from his earliest writings and his work on pensions with Liberal Party bodies during the 1940s, he showed great interest in the attempts by successive governments to establish a 'welfare state' – all of which Seldon thought were doomed to failure. Seldon saw the welfare state as a major intrusion by government into the capitalist system, and one that seriously disadvantaged not just the system as a whole but the poor.

Most likely, he was considerably influenced not only by economic reasoning but also by his own childhood experiences (described in Part I above), surrounded by poor families, where he saw self-help and voluntary community provision at work. Commenting on the provision that his stepfather, Marks Slaberdain, had made for his mother on his death, Seldon remarked:

> … I learned that, far from government having to do such things, the ordinary people were learning because of their consciousness of their own selves, of their wives, dependants and so on. And from that, I think, I must have learned the early beginnings of my suspicion that

government was doing far too much, and that it should leave people, even if they did come from below, to do things for themselves.[1]

The welfare state, he wrote, treats people like '... children who have no power to choose or make or have a view'.[2] On another occasion, in November 1967, he wrote to Lord Balniel, a Conservative peer who had made a speech advocating the integration of cash and care in welfare policy, in similar vein and in very forthright terms, as follows:

> You have never been poor. I have. The poor do not thank those who bring them gifts in kind which question their capacity and affront their dignity. Cash gives the power of choice; care, service in kind, denies choice. But much more than that; the poor who are given care or kind will never *learn* choice, judgement, discrimination, responsibility. To give cash is to take risks but they are the risks the child takes when he learns to walk. Only the mentally or otherwise incapable of learning choice by using cash should be given care or kind.[3]

There is a remarkable consistency in his writings over the years on the welfare state, spanning the period from 1959 to 1998. His work is bold and far sighted, with a contemporary feel, since it deals with fundamental issues that still dog the welfare state, 50 years after Seldon started writing about it. Moreover, for many years he was virtually alone in the views he expressed. As Ralph Harris pointed out, '[he] has fought at times almost single-handed against political complacency and all-party conservatism to compel reconsideration of the assumptions on which universalist welfare policies were perched'.[4] Volume 6 of *The Collected Works* includes eight articles and one book in which the Seldon critique of welfare provision by the state appears. Volume 4 includes six publications that propose means of introducing market forces into 'public' services.

Diagnosis

The Seldon critique is simple yet devastating. Under capitalism, some people will be poor, some of them through no fault of their own. But universal state welfare cannot be the solution to the problem of poverty. It is indiscriminate, providing benefits for the middle classes instead of concentrating on those who genuinely need help. It has adverse effects both on the supply and the demand sides. A direct effect on supply is that welfare services that would have been provided voluntarily are no longer supplied (or the supply is restricted) because it is assumed that welfare is a state responsibility and 'government will provide'. Incentives to save for the future – so as to provide for education, medical needs and generally for one's family – are reduced, and so is community provision of welfare. There are also wider supply-side effects. Because welfare is financed through the tax system, taxes are higher than they otherwise would be and incentives to work are damaged. As Seldon puts it in a 1959 article in which he argues for the gradual withdrawal of state welfare, it is a crutch that people do not need.[5] Furthermore, the administrative costs of the associated bureaucracy are likely to be higher than in the case of private provision. The problem of reduced supply that the system creates is accentuated because, by providing services free at the point of delivery, it generates excess demand. People do not provide for themselves and for others in their communities and become reliant on the state, which, because demand always exceeds supply at the zero price, fights a constant but vain battle to raise the tax revenue that it thinks might permit it to keep up with what consumers want. To control demand, it has to use administrative rationing, such as waiting lists for hospital services.

As Seldon stresses through all his writings on the welfare state, once the state starts to provide welfare services they become difficult to stop. As incomes rise, people should be capable of making their own provision and the welfare state should decline. In practice, however, once governments have control of services they are reluctant to let go. Seldon quotes, with approval, in several of his articles on the welfare state, some prophetic words of the famous British economist Alfred Marshall, who told the 1893 Royal Commission on the Aged Poor that he did not approve of universal pension schemes because 'they do not contain in themselves the seeds of their own disappearance. I am afraid that, if started, they would tend to become perpetual'.[6]

Pensions were a particular interest of Seldon's. In a very bold 1960 IEA paper, *Pensions for Prosperity*, he takes as his starting point Marshall's comment on universal pension schemes. He goes on to argue that private provision is inherently superior and that there should be a move away from the philosophy of state dependence that then prevailed in both the Labour and the Conservative parties. The proposals then being made by the government were, says Seldon, 'conceived in fear, composed in haste, adopted in ignorance'.[7] Seldon proposed a detailed pro-gramme for a gradual transition from dependence to independ-ence which would encourage private provision for retirement and would wind up National Insurance over a period.

On the wider topic of 'universalism' in welfare, Seldon was concerned that it led to 'equal treatment of people in unequal circumstances'.[8] The universalist principle is wasteful and the state will never be able to raise sufficient revenue to satisfy it. Instead, in a 1967 article, 'The future of the welfare state',[9] Seldon sets out a programme of staged reform that would give more to the needy, provide choice and reduce taxation.

When the British National Health Service had its twentieth anniversary in 1968, Seldon published some thoughts on the state of the NHS and its future. In a statement that still seemed topical when the NHS celebrated its sixtieth anniversary in 2008, Seldon remarks that 'its major emerging disadvantage' is that 'the state has been unable to raise enough tax revenue to provide medical care at rising standards'.[10] A market in health-care is indispensable if people's demands are to be met. He describes how such a market could be established, with private insurance having the primary role but with the state acting 'as a long-stop for the exceptionally chronic, the exceptionally costly and the exceptionally poor'.[11]

Given Seldon's views on the welfare state, he was occasionally drawn into controversies about particular current issues. There was such a case in 1970 when he published *The Great Pensions 'Swindle'*.[12] 'Swindle' was a word that had been used by politicians in both major British parties when referring to each other's pension plans. Seldon was incensed at the proposals in the 1969 National Superannuation and Social Insurance Bill, which would, he argued, ensure that instead of people having occupational pension schemes they would become dependent on the state at retirement. Again he argues for reforms that would encourage voluntary saving for retirement and the winding up of compulsory National Insurance.

Following these early writings, Seldon returned on several occasions to analysis of the welfare state and its failings. He argued that there had been a 'lost century' – a period in which government had taken over from markets that had been developing successfully in health, pensions, unemployment and other benefits and had crowded out these promising ventures, replacing them with ineffective and inefficient state-provided welfare. Compulsory provision of services such as education, medicine, housing and pensions had been an attempt to create 'equality by coercion'[13] and had been a wrong turning. In *Wither the Welfare State* in 1981,[14] he says that in the long run the welfare state must wither away because the only way to maintain it would be by a degree of government coercion that the electorate would not tolerate.

A volume published by the IEA in 1996, *Re-privatising Welfare: After the Lost Century*, which Seldon edited, gave him the opportunity to look back on the growth of the welfare state and on his own writings on the subject.[15] He points out that his efforts over 40 years to urge fundamental reform had fallen on deaf ears. The welfare state is, he says, a 'political artefact' with huge opportunity costs because of the better welfare it suppresses. Without it, markets would probably have continued to evolve to provide, for example, education, healthcare, pensions, housing and unemployment insurance, all tailored to meet the needs of individuals. The obstacles to change are political. As in other writings, he warns the politicians to beware because citizens will find means of escape as they become increasingly unwilling to tolerate second-rate services. As Seldon explains in another paper on the future of the welfare state written in the late 1990s, 'The retreat of the state in social welfare', 'It [the state] is retreating too slowly. The subjects are rebelling. And they will continue to rebel until government retreats sufficiently to liberate the freedoms created by economic advance.'[16]

It is a message that politicians are still reluctant to accept. For the last 25 years, both Conservative and Labour governments in Britain have tried to solve the problems of the welfare state by tinkering with the details. Arthur Seldon had been telling them for decades that only root-and-branch reforms, with a return to private sector provision, would be effective.

Remedies

Seldon's solution to the accumulating problems of state welfare was to harness the power of price. He was impressed by the ability of the price system to link buyers and sellers. Without it, he pointed out, the principal means of determining preferences is absent and allocation of scarce resources has to be carried out by politicians and bureaucrats who are necessarily in a state of ignorance about what consumers want. Alongside his critique of the welfare state, he therefore had constructive proposals about how welfare and other services provided by the state would better be provided by markets in which buyers and sellers interacted and prices were established. A book and several papers on the market provision of services are included in Volume 4 of *The Collected Works*.

The essence of Seldon's case is that non-market provision of services by the state leads to a disconnection between suppliers and consumers. Suppliers are financed by taxpayers, rather than directly by consumers of their products, and therefore have no reason to discover what their consumers want now, nor do they have an incentive to innovate to meet future demands. Because suppliers face no competition, there are no rivals to set efficiency standards: inefficient provision is the result. On the demand side, there are also adverse effects. Consumers see a price of zero at the point of service delivery and so their demands expand well beyond what they would have been had they been charged a price that covered the cost of the service. The mismatch between supply and demand is not automatically corrected, because the price mechanism does not operate, and so a bureaucracy, insulated from market forces, carries out the rationing. As Seldon perceptively points out, one unfortunate side effect is that over time this bureaucracy develops a high-handed attitude towards its customers, treating them as though they were supplicants asking for favours. His comment will still ring true with 'customers' of the National Health Service and other state-run services.

Yet there is no reason why so many services should be supplied by the state. Seldon accepts that there may be some 'public' goods and services that the private sector would not supply (either at all, or in the 'right' quantities). But Seldon maintains that most government expenditure is not directed at 'public' goods and services. The state has taken over supply in many areas where private markets are feasible and desirable, and indeed in many cases once existed (as, for instance, in welfare services, as explained above). To provide evidence, in several papers Seldon analyses British government expenditure in detail to determine the extent of genuine public good provision.

The most notable example of such an analysis is in a book, *Charge*, published in 1977, which as the name implies is about charging for goods and services that at the time were supplied by the government. Seldon separates the main items of government expenditure into those that are 'public goods' in the economist's sense (such as defence), those in which some benefits are private (for instance, roads and public lighting) and those in which most of the benefits are private (for example, education, health and housing). He concludes from his analysis that only about one third of government spending is on goods and services that necessarily must be financed by taxes. Most state services therefore 'yield separable private services that could be more efficiently financed by charges'.[17] Seldon explains in some detail in the book how charging could be introduced and how consumers and suppliers would benefit. Another benefit is that government would be kept down to an appropriate size, as Seldon explains in another paper ('Micro-economic controls – disciplining the state by pricing'[18]).

A means of promoting market forces in the provision of state services on which both Arthur Seldon and his wife, Marjorie, were keen was the voucher. In the case of education, they saw an opportunity in the 1980s to introduce vouchers as a means of depoliticising education, introducing choice and competition. The Seldons had many powerful advocates on their side, and they produced a cogent case for the education voucher which appeared to convince the responsible minister, the then Secretary of State for Education, Sir Keith (later Lord) Joseph. Nevertheless, their attempt failed.

One of Seldon's IEA papers, *The Riddle of the Voucher*, published in 1986,[19] is devoted to a discussion of the education voucher, the attempt to persuade the Thatcher government to introduce it and the eventual failure to do so, which he ascribed to the power of producer interests and opposition from the civil service. Intellectual arguments are not enough, concludes Seldon. The episode of the voucher can, as he says, only be understood in terms of public choice theory, which emphasises the power of organised interest groups to influence government policy. Both the teachers and the civil servants thought they had too much to lose from a move to a regime in which consumer choice prevailed. Consumers were not sufficiently organised, nor did they wield sufficient power to persuade the government to accept a policy that would have been greatly to their benefit.

Seldon's writings on charging for public services, like those on the deficiencies of the welfare state, were consistent over many years, and they gave a clear and simple message which, unfortunately, was unpalatable to governments and the relevant interest groups because reliance on markets would have led to loss of their power. Seldon argued that tax-financed provision of services restricts supply, inflates demand and reduces quality. People should have their purchasing power restored by tax reductions and, if necessary, by specific measures such as vouchers. They will then act as consumers, and suppliers will compete to satisfy their demands. Efficiency in provision will improve. Furthermore, says Seldon, people will regain the incentive to provide for themselves instead of relying on the state. It is a message that has still not been accepted by British politicians, who are forever trying to apply 'sticking plaster' remedies to a broken welfare state. Seldon would be telling them to be more radical.

In conclusion

This book began by explaining that Arthur Seldon, who was born into a poor Jewish East End family in the middle of World War I, rose to become a man of great influence who helped to change the climate of ideas about economic and social policy in the last two decades of the twentieth century. He had strong views, based on rigorous analysis, about the benefits for the economy and the community of a capitalist system in which individuals are free to make their choices in competitive markets. Such a regime, he argued, cannot be matched by government 'planning', which, by definition, can never gather the information that would be necessary for it to succeed, and anyway does not embody the incentives that could lead to success.

His influence came not only from the power of his ideas but from his ability to express them succinctly, without resort to technical jargon, in terms that 'opinion-leaders' could understand, and in his ability to draw conclusions for policy. He was not only a prolific writer, with one of the major works of classical liberalism of recent times (*Capitalism*) to his credit, he was also a splendid editor of the work of others, with the ability to formulate a publishing programme with a clear purpose, to find authors to carry it through and to make their work more understandable.

Seldon believed, with Böhm-Bawerk, that economic forces are so strong that they will eventually overcome political power, whatever the obstacles. But Seldon also believed that prominent individuals can hasten the day when economic forces triumph. He seems to have been thinking mainly of politicians such as

Margaret Thatcher and Ronald Reagan, both of whom had deep-seated beliefs in the benefits of markets and the determination to press ahead, in the face of substantial opposition, with the necessary reforms. But though, by choice, he was no politician, Seldon was himself one of those prominent individuals who make change happen. Without his fertile brain, his imagination, his determination, his clear prose and his productive partnership with Ralph Harris, it is most unlikely that the near-worldwide economic transformation that has taken place in the last three decades — away from planning and towards markets — could have occurred.

His family and his many friends remember Arthur's more personal characteristics — his integrity, his tolerance, his loyalty, his warmth, his humour, his willingness and ability to engage with, to teach and to encourage young people. Throughout his long life he set a marvellous example to others, as husband, father, friend and intellectual entrepreneur. His personal qualities helped him to overcome the difficult circumstances of his early years and to leave behind a legacy of major achievements, powerful ideas (some of which still await acceptance) and happy memories of a remarkable man.

Appendix 1

Selected family documents

This appendix contains four documents which are referred to in Chapter 1, all of which are of interest in the context of Arthur Seldon's early years.

First is the adoption certificate of 12 October 1918 which refers to Arthur's adoption by Marks Slaberdain (or Slabadain) and includes the commitment to give the infant Arthur a good education.

Second is the certificate of the marriage of Eva Marks to Simon Finkelstein on 12 April 1931.

Third are two extracts (the first and last pages) from a hand-written essay which Arthur (then Slaberdain) produced in January 1934, entitled 'Some Reflections on the Science of Political Economy'.

The final document is the change of name deed of 1 August 1939, in which Arthur changed his surname from Slaberdain to Seldon.

Arthur Seldon's adoption certificate, 12 October 1918

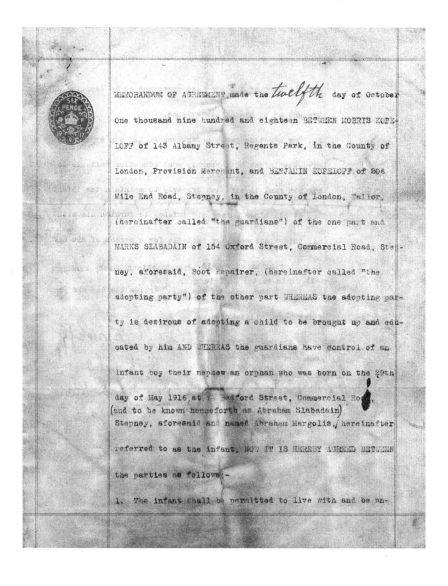

MEMORANDUM OF AGREEMENT made the *twelfth* day of October One thousand nine hundred and eighteen BETWEEN MORRIS KOPE-LOFF of 143 Albany Street, Regents Park, in the County of London, Provision Merchant, and BENJAMIN KOPELOFF of 206 Mile End Road, Stepney, in the County of London, Tailor, (hereinafter called "the guardians") of the one part and MARKS SLABADAIN of 154 Oxford Street, Commercial Road, Step-ney, aforesaid, Boot Repairer, (hereinafter called "the adopting party") of the other part WHEREAS the adopting par-ty is desirous of adopting a child to be brought up and edu-cated by him AND WHEREAS the guardians have control of an infant boy their nephew an orphan who was born on the 29th day of May 1916 at Bedford Street, Commercial Road, (and to be known henceforth as Abraham Slabadain) Stepney, aforesaid and named Abraham Margolis, hereinafter referred to as the infant, NOW IT IS HEREBY AGREED BETWEEN the parties as follows:-

1. The infant shall be permitted to live with and be un-

der the care of the adopting party and to be educated and

brought up by him at his expense.

2. The adopting party undertakes at his own expense to

give the infant a thoroughly good education suitable to

his own rank in life and properly to maintain the infant

and at all times during his infancy to furnish him with

all things necessary or suitable for a person of his age

in such rank as aforesaid. The Guardians hereby renounce
all claim to the said infant.
AS WITNESS the hands of the said parties the day and year

first above written.

WITNESS to the signatures of)
the said Morris Kopeloff
Benjamin Kopeloff and
Marks Slabadain. —
A. Colville Blumer.
Solicitor,
221 Bishopsgate,
E.C.2

M. Kopeloff

B. Kopeloff

M. Slabadain

Eva and Simon Finkelstein's marriage certificate, 12 April 1931

ABSTRACT OF THE כְּתוּבָה

On the *First* day of the week, the *Twenty fifth*
day of the month *Nison* , in the year 569 *1* , A.M.,
corresponding to the *12ᵗʰ* day of the month in the
year 193*1* , the holy Covenant of Marriage was entered into, in
London, between the Bridegroom— *Simon Finkelstein*

and his Bride— *Eva Haladin* .

The said Bridegroom made the following declaration to his
Bride:

"Be thou my wife according to the law of Moses and of
Israel. I faithfully promise that I will be a true husband unto
thee. I will honour and cherish thee; I will work for thee; I
will protect and support thee, and will provide all that is
necessary for thy due sustenance, even as it beseemeth a Jewish
husband to do. I also take upon myself all such further
obligations for thy maintenance, during thy life-time, as are
prescribed by our religious statute."

And the said Bride has plighted her troth unto him, in
affection and with sincerity, and has thus taken upon herself the
fulfilment of all the duties incumbent upon a Jewish wife.

This Covenant of Marriage was duly executed and
witnessed this day according to the usage of Israel.

Handwritten essay by Arthur Seldon, January 1934 (first and last pages)

1.

January 1934.

Some Reflections on the Science of Political Economy

1. Introduction
2. Personal Reactions.
3. Economics and General Education
4. Economics and Politics.
5. Economics and 'Other Subjects'
6. Prof. Robbins and "Homo Œconomicus".
7. Economic Theory through the Ages.
8. Economics Examinations.
9. Laissez Faire and 'Economic Planning'
10. Conclusion.

I have searched the dictionary in the hope of finding a word or phrase to summarise my reactions after two years of study of Economics; I have failed. The reason, be it noted, is not my lack of power of concentration in failing to look through all the dictionary, nor the fallibility of the dictionarists in failing to provide a suitable word, but simply the inconsistency of my reactions.

At one time, peculiar as it may first appear, I despise anyone who cannot explain changes in the rate of interest, or who exclaims, "Why doesn't the government make work for the unemployed?" I feel that anyone who is ignorant of the elementary basic principles of Economics is superfluous and should be painlessly destroyed. And yet someone had the audacity to attempt to prove to me that tariffs make work! Previously I had regarded this person

7.

A. Slabberdain.

princes which one reads as a child. Later I became a rabid fiery Socialist. I find now that my opinions were based on sentiment and snobbishness — on the observation of the conditions under which some of the less fortunate members of society of lived. The study of economics has not only exposed the fallacy of the absurd opinions which I once held, but has also even prejudiced me against my former political friends. The study of Economics has been the cause of my moving to the Right. Will I change again? I wonder.........

Well worth reading.

Arthur Seldon's change of name deed, 1 August 1939

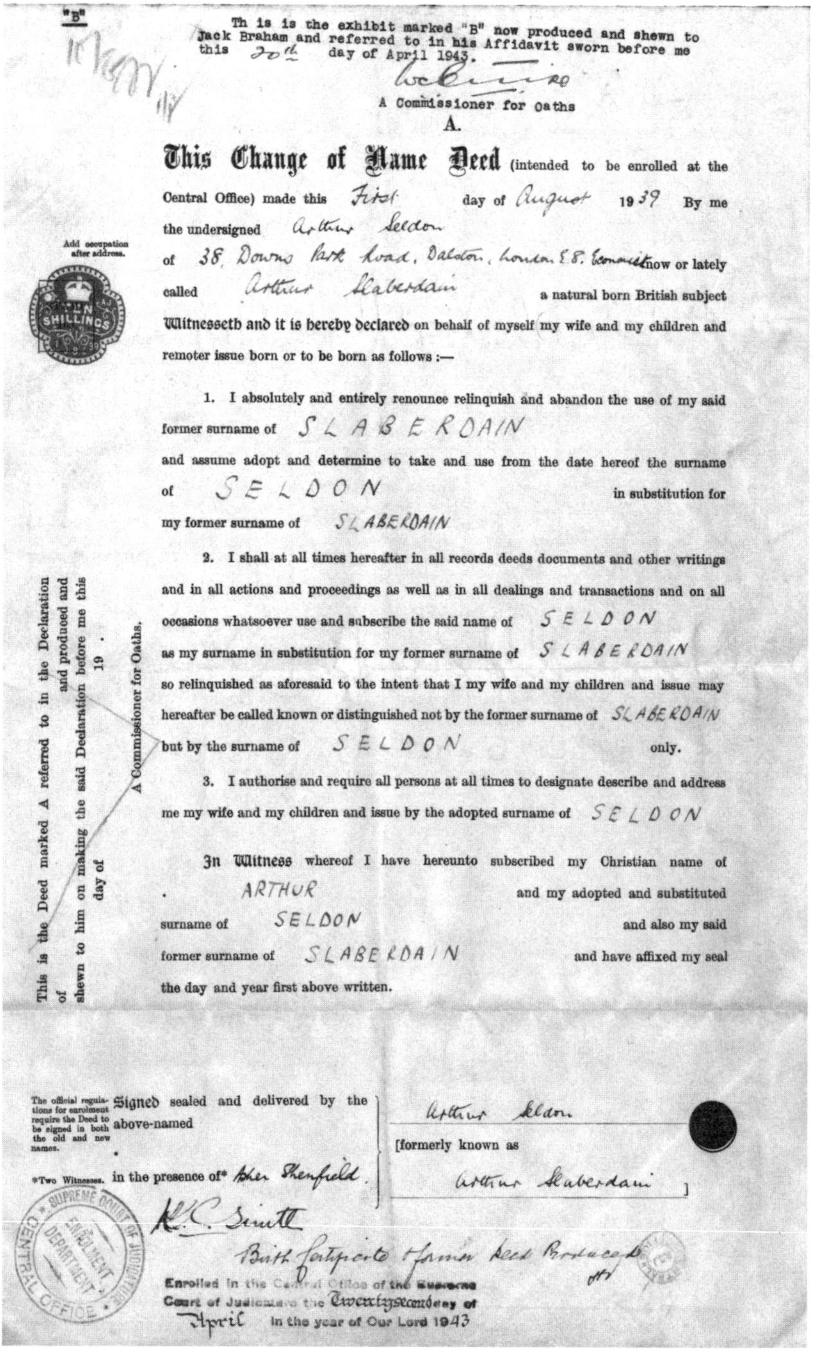

"B"

This is the exhibit marked "B" now produced and shewn to Jack Braham and referred to in his Affidavit sworn before me this 20th day of April 1943.

A Commissioner for Oaths

A.

This Change of Name Deed (intended to be enrolled at the Central Office) made this First day of August 1939 By me the undersigned Arthur Seldon of 38, Downs Park Road, Dalston, London E.8. Economist now or lately called Arthur Slaberdain a natural born British subject

Add occupation after address.

Witnesseth and it is hereby declared on behalf of myself my wife and my children and remoter issue born or to be born as follows :—

1. I absolutely and entirely renounce relinquish and abandon the use of my said former surname of SLABERDAIN and assume adopt and determine to take and use from the date hereof the surname of SELDON in substitution for my former surname of SLABERDAIN

2. I shall at all times hereafter in all records deeds documents and other writings and in all actions and proceedings as well as in all dealings and transactions and on all occasions whatsoever use and subscribe the said name of SELDON as my surname in substitution for my former surname of SLABERDAIN so relinquished as aforesaid to the intent that I my wife and my children and issue may hereafter be called known or distinguished not by the former surname of SLABERDAIN but by the surname of SELDON only.

3. I authorise and require all persons at all times to designate describe and address me my wife and my children and issue by the adopted surname of SELDON

In Witness whereof I have hereunto subscribed my Christian name of ARTHUR and my adopted and substituted surname of SELDON and also my said former surname of SLABERDAIN and have affixed my seal the day and year first above written.

This is the Deed marked A referred to in the Declaration of and produced and shewn to him on making the said Declaration before me this day of 19 .

A Commissioner for Oaths.

The official regulations for enrolment require the Deed to be signed in both the old and new names.

Signed sealed and delivered by the above-named Arthur Seldon [formerly known as Arthur Slaberdain]

Two Witnesses. in the presence of Asher Shenfield

Both footprints & former deed produced

Enrolled in the Central Office of the Supreme Court of Judicature the Twentysecond day of April in the year of Our Lord 1943

SUPREME COURT OF JUDICATURE ENROLMENT DEPARTMENT CENTRAL OFFICE

Arthur (at left) with Prime Minister Margaret Thatcher and Ralph Harris

Arthur with Lee Kuan Yew, Prime Minister of Singapore, 22 February 1980

Ralph Harris, Arthur and Friedrich Hayek outside the Institute of Economic Affairs in Lord North Street, mid 1980s

Arthur and Marjorie outside Buckingham Palace after receiving his CBE on 30 November 1983

Above: Arthur with Martin Anderson at Lord North Street, mid 1990s

Right: Daniel Doron (at left) and Milton Friedman. Arthur gave great encouragement to Daniel Doron, the director of the Israel Centre for Economic Social Progress, who often visited Arthur in England

The distinguished economist W. H. (Bill) Hutt and his wife Grethe
with Arthur at the IEA in the mid 1980s

The ceremony of nomination of Arthur as the first Honorary Fellow
of the Mont Pelerin Society at the Vienna conference, September
1996. From left: Dr Edwin Feulner, Professor Pascal Salin, Ralph
Harris and Arthur

Arthur and Marjorie on holiday in Scotland in September 1981

Three brothers: (left to right) Sidney, Cecil and Arthur in the mid 1980s

Arthur singing 'My Heart's Delight' at his golden wedding
anniversary party at the Charing Cross Hotel on 23 February 1998.
Holding the music is the opera singer Mandy Pomorski

Arthur (at right)
with Professor
Colin Robinson
at the Institute of
Economic Affairs
50th anniversary
celebration at the
Reform Club,
June 2005

Arthur Seldon, 1916–2005

Appendix 2

Major awards to Arthur Seldon

Arthur Seldon received many awards during his lifetime. The five most significant awards are listed below, in the order in which he received them

- Commander of the Order of the British Empire (CBE): 1983
- Fellow of the Mont Pelerin Society: 1996. (Seldon was the first person to be made an Honorary Fellow of the MPS.)
- Honorary Doctorate, La Universidad Francisco Marroquín, Guatemala: 1998
- Honorary Doctorate, University of Buckingham: 1999
- Fellow of the London School of Economics and Political Science (LSE): 2001

Appendix 3

Tributes to Arthur Seldon

Following are two of the tributes to Arthur Seldon given at his memorial service on 15 January 2006, and which appeared (along with a number of others) in the IEA's journal, *Economic Affairs*, 26(2), June 2006, under the heading 'Arthur Seldon: great editor, thinker and radical economist'. Two of the other tributes were by Stuart Waterhouse and Martin Anderson. They are not included here because they overlap with the contributions to this book made by Waterhouse and Anderson.

A tribute to a friend and colleague
Ralph Harris (Lord Harris of High Cross)

I hardly trust myself to speak in public of both my love for Arthur Seldon and my debt to him. He was at once a colleague, a teacher, an inspirer – and a constant, delightful, whimsical companion over 30 years at the IEA, plus a bonus of fifteen years in shared retirement. He rescued me from a youthful infatuation with party politics; and showed how we could, together, stick to our last, as independent missionaries of our classical liberal inheritance, imbibed by him under Robbins, Plant and Hayek at the LSE and by me under Robertson, Dennison and Prest at Cambridge, before the Keynesians took over.

By happy chance, we shared similar roots in respectable working-class families – him in the East End of London and me a few miles north in Tottenham. We both made our ways from state elementary and grammar schools, before being (as he might say) 'propelled' by scholarships to university.

In 1957 Antony Fisher became our shared patron, setting us up at the Institute of Economic Affairs in harmonious and fruitful partnership. I might almost claim to have rescued Arthur from demon drink, since he was then working as economic adviser to the brewing industry. If he were given to similar flights of fancy, he might claim to have rescued me from working out life tenure at a sleepy Scottish university.

Almost fifty years later, in October, a quite remarkable crop of obituaries bore unanimous witness to his reputation and international fame. As master editor, he had assembled a formidable army of mostly younger market economists, though headed by Hayek and Friedman. Proof of the unique authority he acquired was that when Hayek feared ill health might prevent him completing his trilogy – *Law, Legislation* and *Liberty* – he instructed his secretary that in such an event he wished Arthur to take over its completion.

Arthur's own legacy is glimpsed not only in his recently published volumes of collected works, plus his powerful journalism, but in a veritable library of scholarly IEA papers that helped overthrow the ruling post-war Keynesian collectivist consensus. More positively, he reasserted the primacy of dispersed market forces as the prime mover of all enduring economic and social progress in a free society.

Influence at arm's length – Arthur Seldon's influence on policymaking and politicians
Geoffrey Howe (Lord Howe of Aberavon, former Chancellor of the Exchequer and Foreign Secretary)

This is a truly daunting privilege – to pay tribute to Arthur, from the perspective, in Adam Smith's words, of 'that crafty and insidious animal, vulgarly called "a politician"'. For on the face of it, Arthur had no use for the likes of me. 'Good men', he once said, 'are induced by the political process to do harm.' For him, we were, and I quote him again, 'the fundamental obstacle' to necessary change. So it must be the supreme irony that Arthur has now been identified, by one obituarist after another, as 'the intellectual progenitor of the Thatcher revolution ... almost single-handedly responsible for overturning an entire political consensus'.

Certainly not single-handed, of course. Antony Fisher, Ralph Harris and, above all, Marjorie Seldon were indispensable partners. And certainly not by becoming a politician himself – but by seeking to permeate and transform much wider public attitudes. And permeate the body politic he certainly did. My (slightly younger) generation of Bow Group Conservatives were fascinated by the candid clarity of his analysis and the modesty of his magnetism (he was one of the first Hobart Place authors to write for our brave, quarterly magazine – *Crossbow*). For exactly the same reasons, and from the earliest days, much more powerful figures than us – Douglas Houghton (Chairman of the Parliamentary Labour Party), for example, Jo Grimond, Enoch Powell and, far from least, Keith Joseph – were all eager disciples.

And Arthur was certainly not averse to political proselytisation. Way back in 1969, he sought my view of Margaret Thatcher as a possible target for the Institute. My response was 'cautiously encouraging' – which was just as well. For on Arthur's death Margaret had this to say: 'his visionary work inspired much of our success'.

Arthur was, very self-consciously, a Liberal – and he enjoyed emphasising that, above all, particularly to Tory politicians. We were only too happy to forgive him! And we are grateful too, for being able to join in saluting his memory and achievements here today.

Appendix 4

Obituaries

The founding fathers of the Institute of Economic Affairs, Arthur Seldon and Ralph Harris, were for long widely regarded as political crackpots. Their advocacy in the 1960s and 1970s of free-market economics and pricing for public services was dismissed even by the Conservative Party. By the early 1980s, however, they gradually began to win over the political establishment. It is a remarkable story of the power of ideas.

It was to the IEA that Sir Keith Joseph turned, in his own words, 'for an education' in free-market economics, following the Conservative general election defeat in February 1974. Those meetings led to the creation of the Centre for Policy Studies, development of Thatcherism, and the frontal assault on the post-war collectivist consensus.

The great Austrian economist Joseph Schumpeter had warned in 1942 that capitalism would decline because it did not have persuasive defenders. Businessmen lacked charisma and were too busy seeking favours from government in the form of subsidies and restricting competition. The case for the free market and profits paled beside that of planning and social justice. Even as Prime Minister, Margaret Thatcher still complained in private that capitalism was discredited in schools, universities, churches and media. The IEA may have been a voice in the wilderness in the 1960s but, as she often acknowledged, it prepared the path for Thatcherism.

Seldon was born in the East End of London in 1916 and had few advantages. He was orphaned at the age of three (his parents died of Spanish flu) and then adopted by a childless cobbler and his wife. A legacy of that experience was his strong belief in self-help. To the end of his life he complained that the bureaucratically managed welfare state and priceless goods and services, supplied 'free' by the Government, discouraged independence and self-esteem among its clients.

He wanted people to receive money and vouchers so that they could choose their own schools and hospital treatment.

That would encourage their commitment to self-improvement and independence and break the power of 'bossy' bureaucrats and welfare providers. Indeed state welfare actually undermined the traditional forms of self-help, through the community, charities and friendly societies. His Judaism reinforced these beliefs.

Seldon's scholarship to the London School of Economics was decisive for his intellectual development. He embraced the classical liberal economics, taught by Professors Lionel Robbins, Friedrich Hayek and Arnold Plant, rather than the Fabianism found elsewhere in the school. In 1940 Plant headed a small survey research unit at the Ministry of Information and for a time employed the young Seldon to draw up the sampling frame for interviews. After the Second World War, in which he served in the Army in Africa and Italy, Seldon taught evening classes at the LSE, and conducted research for the brewery industry.

Harris was put in by the entrepreneur Antony Fisher as General Director of the IEA in 1957 and Seldon as part-time editor soon after. They were an unlikely combination. Harris, the front man, was confident, colourful, moustachioed, and often sported a bow tie and bright shirt. Seldon dressed soberly, was short, stocky and studious and cursed with a terrible stammer that limited his public role. The impediment meant that he shone in print not on the platform. At their first meeting Harris wondered how such a retiring person would fare in an entrepreneurial body. Both men kept clear of party politics, though Seldon was a traditional Liberal. But it was the free-market wing of the Conservative Party that was most sympathetic to their ideas.

The first 30 years of the IEA were inseparable from the personalities of Seldon and Harris. It was organised in 1957 as a research and educational trust – today it would be called a think tank. For a time it attracted the support of only the non-Keynesian economists and Conservatives disillusioned with the collectivist drift of the party; at the time both were beleaguered minorities. It promoted and published the work of Milton Friedman and Friedrich Hayek on monetarism and markets. Indeed Seldon regularly edited and polished the work of the latter.

The job of commissioning, reviewing and editing (he ruthlessly excised jargon) over 350 papers and pamphlets was a demanding one. Many young authors owed their first start to Seldon's skills in developing neglected topics and fussily transforming first drafts into polished prose. The pamphlets and seminars were aimed at the informed public in the belief that shaping the climate of opinion was the best way of influencing politicians.

Seldon actually wrote the first IEA pamphlet in 1957, *Pensions in a Free Society*. It argued for personal private pensions, something achieved 30 years later. Although he was a generous man and interested in new ideas, the years of derision and indifference from politicians and media left a mark on him. Sympathetic politicians (like the young Geoffrey Howe, Enoch Powell or Sir Keith Joseph in 1964) were treasured as 'a friend' or 'a supporter'. For a time there was something of an 'us and them' attitude.

Over time, and particularly after 1979, Seldon and Harris saw many of their supposedly eccentric ideas carried into policy, including privatisation, control of the money supply, creation of an independent university, student loans, trade-union reforms etc. But there were setbacks. He and his wife, Marjorie, were ardent supporters of school vouchers and had high hopes that Sir Keith Joseph, the Secretary of State for Education between 1981 and 1986, would promote the idea. They were disappointed when he accepted the objections of his civil servants and aghast that his education reforms resulted in such central control of schools and universities. Thatcher's NHS reforms also found no place for health vouchers.

Seldon saw little point in curbing the power of the producers, only to increase that of politicians and bureaucrats. The market was more responsive to popular choice than the political process. Genuine reform should empower consumers and customers. Seldon always took the long view and believed that his ideas would win out eventually.

The relationship between Harris and Seldon, although

fruitful, was not without its strains. Seldon, overshadowed by his more high-profile partner, was not pleased that Harris was singled out for a peerage in 1979 (he took the title Lord Harris of High Cross). Many in the IEA were embarrassed and regarded it as a slight to Seldon; it seemed invidious to distinguish their contributions. His life was the IEA and he looked askance at Harris's fund-raising on behalf of the Mont Pelerin Society and the private University of Buckingham. Seldon was bored with Europe, while Harris was a passionate Eurosceptic. Their shared vision and sense of achievement overcame these differences.

Seldon retired as Editorial Director in 1981 but remained as a very active consultant editor until 1988. A year later Harris resigned. They disagreed over the appointment of Harris's successor. Seldon did not regard Graham Mather, who wanted to target the policy makers more directly and tackle wider issues, as the appropriate choice as General Director. Both agreed, however, that the IEA under Mather was becoming too close to John Major. After clashes Mather resigned in 1992.

Arthur Seldon was a remarkable spotter of young authors. He brought politicians and intellectuals together at lunches at the Lord North Street offices, acquired in 1969. He encouraged his contributors to follow their own ideas and 'think the unthinkable'.

His years as editor held him back from his own writing. But he became productive in his later period and his publications include *The Great Pensions Swindle* (1970), *Charge* (1977), *Capitalism* (1990), *The State is Rolling Back* (1994: essays spanning 50 years), *The Dilemma of Democracy* (1998) and *The Making of the IEA* (2002). His death comes on the eve of the publication of the seventh and final volume of his collected works.

The Seldons had three sons. Anthony, the youngest, is author of acclaimed biographies of John Major and Tony Blair; he inherited much of his father's editorial and networking talents but not his politics.

Arthur and his remarkable wife, Marjorie (whose uncle

invented daylight saving), continued to host social and intellectual gatherings at their home ('The Thatched Cottage') outside
Sevenoaks. He liked to call them 'parties for non-conformists'.

Dennis Kavanagh

Arthur Seldon was one of the most powerful exponents of classical liberalism in the second half of the 20th century – both as
writer and editor. He was one of the great editors. He was constantly seeking authors who would pursue ideas to their logical
conclusion, no matter how radical the ensuing reform proposals.
Authors' initial efforts would be peppered with suggestions for
change, particularly if the ideas were not clearly expressed
without technical jargon and if (the ultimate sin) reform proposals were trimmed to take account of the 'politically acceptable'.

At the same time he was a prolific author, starting at the age
of 21 and producing 28 books and some 230 articles. His work,
ranging from long books to short newspaper pieces, has been
gathered by Liberty Fund of Indianapolis under the title *The
Collected Works of Arthur Seldon*. The *Collected Works* is full of
original ideas and genuinely accessible to people with no formal
training in economics. His analysis, from the late 1950s onwards,
of the inherent deficiencies of the welfare state is far ahead of its
time. He was also one of the first to perceive the problem of
over-government in representative political systems where infrequent elections are insufficient to keep politicians and civil servants in check.

Arthur could be impatient – for instance, with the slow pace
of economic reform in Britain in the 1980s and, more generally,
with socialism, which he saw as a system that is fundamentally
misguided and incapable of being mended. But in his personal
dealings he was patience itself.

Summarising the contribution of a person of such stature is
not easy. But the economic and business worlds in Britain and
abroad would be quite different – and much more hostile to
enterprise – without the efforts of Arthur Seldon.

Professor Colin Robinson

The Times, 12 October 2005

Arthur Seldon was a prophet of what came to be called Thatcherism. The Thatcherite revolution of the 1970s and 1980s had many roots, but one was certainly a sea change in the intellectual climate of the times, and Seldon played a huge role in that sea change.

For years the State had been seen as the pre-eminent force in managing the economy and providing social security. Seldon was a tireless advocate of replacing the welfare state and of allowing natural economic laws of supply and demand to increase national wealth more effectively than the man in Whitehall could ever do. Not that he had ever been an enthusiast for the Conservative Party. Fundamentally Seldon was an old-fashioned Liberal who believed in the liberty – and responsibility – of the individual.

The causes he espoused, for replacing state welfare by encouragement of the individual to provide for his own care, were dismissed at the time as eccentric or dangerous. He had the satisfaction as a prophet of seeing his ideas absorbed into political thinking, not just by Thatcher's Conservatives but later by Blair's New Labour. What had been dangerous thinking in the 1960s was accepted as sensible and orthodox in the 1990s.

In the 1960s and 1970s Seldon was a voice in the wilderness as he hit out at the folly of Labour and Conservative politicians alike as they expanded state welfare and fiddled with the economy.

From his desk in the modest offices of the Institute of Economic Affairs (IEA), around the corner from the Houses of Parliament, he strove relentlessly to educate opinion to see that ordinary people's welfare and prosperity would be better served by 'rolling back the State'.

Seldon was born in the East End of London. At the age of 3 he was orphaned – his parents died of the Spanish flu – and he was adopted by a cobbler and his wife. His education began at Dempsey Street Elementary School, Stepney. He went on to

Raine's Foundation School and then to the London School of Economics, where he took a First in 1937.

After the war, during which he served in Africa and Italy, he was editor of the magazine *Store*, where he developed his ideas on the harm done to the economy by the notorious British distaste for commerce and salesmanship and the other trappings of free enterprise. Significantly, his first book (in 1959) was *Advertising in a Free Society*.

Meanwhile, he was active in Liberal politics. He was chairman of the party's committee on the aged in 1948–49, and he took part in one of the most famous by-election campaigns of the century – at Orpington in 1962 – when the Liberals took the seat from the Tories and seriously shook the confidence of the Macmillan Government. From then on, the writing was on the wall for old-style Conservatism. Tories had to rethink their philosophy.

In 1959 Seldon became co-founder and editorial director of the IEA. Sloppy thinkers often dismissed the IEA as a Conservative cover organisation. In fact it was always careful to preserve its independence, and recognised that much of its inspiration came from Liberal doctrines of free trade.

Being limited as a public speaker by a noticeable stutter, Seldon was obliged to expound his ideas in print. As a writer or editor he produced an avalanche of books, pamphlets and articles in newspapers and journals challenging the 'postwar consensus', which had seen the Conservatives accepting many of the doctrines of the Attlee Labour Government.

The IEA's influence among politicians, academics and journalists was enormous. Seldon's part in this helped to change economic opinion abroad as well as in Britain. In his particular specialism, the financing of welfare services, he was in demand as a consultant and adviser. In the late 1960s he was a member of the committee on health financing of the British Medical Association and adviser to the Australian Cabinet committee on welfare.

He fostered exchange of information on how Britain's

welfare state compared with other countries. He became involved with many politico-economic institutes in Europe and the US. From 1980 to 1986 he was vice-president of the respected Mont Pelerin Society – the group, which advocates 'classical liberalism' and free-market economic policies, arose from a conference organised in 1947 by Friedrich Hayek at the Swiss resort of Mont Pelerin.

Much of Seldon's writing was done jointly with the IEA's director and co-founder, Ralph Harris, later Lord Harris of High Cross. The long list of the titles of his books gave the flavour of the message: they included *Choice in Welfare* (1963); *After the NHS* (1968); *The Great Pensions Swindle* (1970).

In an article in *The Times* he once explained how the natural political alignment in British voting was not between Left and Right but between a Minimal State Party ('with a Whiggish flavour') and a Paternalist Party. He was in no doubt that the majority of voters would opt for minimal interference by the State, because they knew better how to run their lives and would spend their own money better than politicians.

The *Daily Telegraph*, 13 October 2005

Arthur Seldon, who died on Tuesday aged 89, was, with Ralph Harris, one of the founders of the Institute of Economic Affairs, the think-tank which advanced free-market ideas at a time when they were deeply out of favour, and which provided much of the intellectual underpinning for Thatcherism.

The success of the IEA was in large part due to Seldon's gifts as an editor, and to the care with which he encouraged young writers. Many proposals which were later to be taken up by politicians might never have seen the light of day without Seldon's meticulous removal of jargon and insistence that the ideas being presented should be comprehensible to a wide audience. Seldon himself had no interest in narrow party politics. He was not a Tory, but an old-fashioned Liberal, and insisted that shaping public attitudes, rather than courting politicians, should be the IEA's priority.

Arthur Seldon was born on May 29 1916 in the East End of London; his parents were Russian-Jewish immigrants who died in the 1918 'flu epidemic and, aged two, young Arthur was adopted by a neighbouring childless cobbler and his wife who had also immigrated from Russia. In later life he recalled helping to sell repaired boots on a Saturday at the market in Whitechapel Road.

This background helped foster his belief in self-reliance. When he was 11, Arthur's adoptive father died, and his widow collected £100 from a Friendly Society. Seldon quoted this as an example of family self-help before it was crowded-out by the welfare state. Likewise, before the era of 'counsellors', his mother consulted neighbours and was helped to make a living by selling lisle stockings at 1s 11¾d a pair from their front room in Oxford Street, E1.

Some years later she married – 'for Arthur's sake' – an elderly tailor with his own workshop, which prospered until the Depression of 1929. From Dempsey Street Elementary, Arthur passed the 11-plus and went on to Raine's Foundation Grammar

School off the Commercial Road (later abolished by Anthony Crosland's comprehensive reorganisation). In 1934 he won a state scholarship to the London School of Economics, where he came under the influence of Lionel Robbins and FA Hayek, who had recently arrived from Vienna. After a brief flirtation with Communism he saw the light and joined a few others in establishing a student Liberal Society.

Despite the dominance of Laski and Dalton, who gave the LSE its undeserved reputation as a hot-house of Socialism, Seldon imbibed there his life-long belief in the commanding tenets of classical liberalism, based on secure property rights and open competitive markets as the foundation of long-run prosperity and individual freedom. After a First in 1937 he became research assistant to Sir Arnold Plant before joining the Army. From 1942 to 1945 he served in North Africa and Italy, emerging unscathed, apart from a stiffened right arm resulting from an infection.

After 1945, Seldon returned to what he always called 'the School', where he tutored part-time students in the commerce degree bureau and was appointed a staff examiner. From 1946 to 1949 he edited a retail trade journal, *Store*, where he met and married Marjorie Perrott (née Willett), whose uncle invented Daylight Saving Time. She was a war widow with a son, whom Arthur adopted.

For the next decade Seldon worked as economic adviser to the brewing industry and found himself gently advising heads of famous family firms that they must improve their amenities at a time when they were vulnerable to take-over bids. He had seen that dividend limitation kept company shares far below the site value of many pubs.

In January 1957, on the initiative of a Liberal peer, Lord Grantchester, Seldon was introduced to Ralph Harris (now Lord Harris of High Cross), who was general director (and sole employee) of the newly-formed, independent Institute of Economic Affairs, of which Seldon soon became editorial director. In a single week-end at the Reform Club he drafted a paper, published a few months' later as *Pensions in a Free Society*. It unfashionably declared: 'The philosophy underlying this paper is that most of us are now adult enough to be left, or to be helped, to live our own lives according to our own lights ... The transition from dependence to independence must be gradual; that is all the more reason for beginning soon.'

There followed a remarkable 30-year partnership between Seldon and Harris that produced more than 300 scholarly books and papers which contributed powerfully, perhaps decisively, to the turn-round in party politics from the Keynesian-collectivist consensus of Butskellism to the market-centred programmes of Thatcher and Blair.

As self-confessed members of the awkward squad, Seldon and Harris were soon writing seminal studies of advertising and hire purchase in the free society series, and later co-authored further reports, including several on public versus private welfare.

The IEA had been set-up as an educational charity by a Sussex farming entrepreneur named Antony Fisher from the early profits of the Buxted Chicken company. While Harris built up the finances and student network of the Institute, Seldon became the incomparable, pro-active editor, orchestrating a rapidly growing academy of scholars, including Hayek, Milton Friedman and several other Nobel Laureates, as well as unknown junior scholars whom he coached to prominence.

Seldon identified not only important, but misunderstood or neglected, topics. After surviving an operation for an ulcer only when his rare blood group – for which stocks were unavailable – was matched to a bus driver from Edgware after a frantic search, he wrote *The Price of Blood* (1964), which argued for the market to be let loose to increase blood supplies.

He matched authors to each subject and urged them to develop analysis with recommendations for policy, but with no regard for what was then thought 'politically impossible'. His aim was to destroy the post-war consensus and rehabilitate the classical liberal philosophy of limited government based on competition and the widest freedom of personal choice.

When faint-hearts dwelt on obstacles to radical reform, he declared that market forces would triumph over the short-term, opportunistic manoeuvres of puny party politicians. Yet despite his unceasing advocacy of the education voucher, in which he was especially helped by a devoted and energetic wife, he was doomed to watch his hopes dashed by mounting spending.

He was a pioneer in Britain of the American 'public choice' school, which led him to confront the frequent cry of 'market failure' with the charge of what he called 'incorrigible government failure'. The trouble he diagnosed was 'that politicians are not generally saints pursuing the long-term public interest, but party politicians responding to demands from organised lobbies'.

For Seldon, the profit motive governed by consumers in an open competitive economy was more truly democratic – and wholesome – than the vote motive operating in a regime of so-called representative government dominated by pressure groups.

His scholarly magnum opus entitled simply *Capitalism* (1990) failed to attract the public attention it deserved. But in his more populist writing he never ceased to challenge all three political parties. 'The ultimate solution is nothing less than the displacement of "public officials" and "public servants" by the revival of the authority of parents to reject inadequate schools, crowded medical centres and captive housing, by empowering them to pay fees, medical insurance or other costs,' he wrote in 2001.

On his 80th birthday, Lady Thatcher wrote to offer her congratulations, declaring that Seldon had made 'an invaluable contribution to the political and economic map of Britain.

'At a time when free enterprise and the free market were unfashionable you championed their cause, laying the foundations for their revival in the 1970s … You always refused to accept Britain's decline and through your visionary work and rigorous preparation, you inspired much of our success during the 1980s.'

Seldon was a Founder Trustee of the Social Affairs Unit, a Vice-President, and the first Honorary Fellow, of the Mont Pelerin Society, an Honorary Fellow of the LSE, and an honorary graduate of the private University of Buckingham – of which he might be regarded as the intellectual begetter. By comparison, many thought the CBE he was awarded in 1983 inadequate recognition of his service as a leading architect of the economic reforms associated with Thatcherism.

Seldon's phenomenal industry continued in his later years, when his books included *The Dilemma of Democracy* and *The Retreat of the State* (both 1998); *Government:Whose obedient servant?* (2000) and *The Making of the IEA* (2002). His work as an author was crowned by the recent publication of his *Collected Works*, in seven volumes, by Liberty Fund of Indianapolis, edited by Professor Colin Robinson, his successor as editorial director at IEA. The final volume is to be launched in December; a conference on his work is to be held next year.

He was fond of cricket and opera, and was particularly noted for the 'parties for non-conformists' which he and Marjorie threw at their house near Sevenoaks.

Arthur Seldon is survived by his wife and by their three sons.

The *Guardian*, 13 October 2005

The economist and writer Arthur Seldon, who has died aged 89, was one of a small band who, in effect, launched what eventually came to be known as the Thatcherite revolution. Together with the entrepreneur the late Sir Antony Fisher and Ralph (now Lord) Harris, he founded the Institute of Economic Affairs (IEA) in 1957.

Seldon participated in the management of the IEA, particularly its vigorous programme of publications, and was its editorial director from 1957 until 1988. During that time the organisation evolved from barely tolerated fringe grouping to pillar of a new, or renewed, orthodoxy which prepared the ground for the politico-ideological Thatcher enterprise launched in 1979.

Seldon was a man of his age. Born in the East End of London during the first world war into the Jewish artisan class, and faithful to his Jewish roots, he was orphaned at the age of three by the influenza epidemic that swept Europe at the close of the first world war. He was adopted by a cobbler and his wife, attended Dempsey Street elementary school in Stepney, and was a state scholar at Raine's foundation school. Seldon benefited from the educational provisions of the time, which enabled him to make his way to the London School of Economics where, in 1937, he graduated with first class honours.

Fleetingly, in 1940, he worked with a Ministry of Information survey research unit, but then served in the army in Africa and Italy from 1942 to 1945. After the war, he edited the periodical *Store*, from 1946 to 1949, while teaching evening classes at the LSE – and from 1956 to 1966 was a staff examiner there. He was also from 1948 to 1949 chairman of a Liberal Party committee on the aged. From 1949 to 1959 he worked as an economist in industry – conducting industrial research – before and alongside his recruitment to the newly-founded IEA, Fisher's brainchild. At first he was a part-time editorial director, but soon it became a full-time post. Meanwhile Harris was appointed general director.

In that job as editorial director, Seldon was personally responsible for commissioning and editing a stream of booklets, periodicals and other publications that played a considerable part in modifying the climate of opinion in Britain. Authors published included Friedrich Hayek and Milton Friedman. The thoroughness and responsibility of this editing made it a heavy workload, but, in addition, he wrote more than two dozen books and 10 times that number of articles in newspapers and periodicals.

The general reader may remember him, and the IEA, best for their macroeconomic polemics. During three decades these transformed the mindset of policymakers and commentators. They were swayed from neo-Keynesian and statist certainties – which rejected disagreement and categorised 'monetarism' as an eighth deadly sin – to a new consensus. This would indeed be called 'monetarist', but that epithet had not then fallen into desuetude, together with the ideas which gave it birth.

However, Seldon's remit ran much wider. From the outset, he advocated what now would be called 'compassionate conservatism'. He demonstrated in a series of works that the working classes were in many ways the principal victims of socialism and welfarism. In 1957 he co-wrote *Pensions in a Free Society*, the IEA's first pamphlet. Two years later came *Advertising in a Free Society*, and in 1960 he co-wrote *Pensions for Prosperity*.

His picture of the working classes was a remembered one, of people capable of self-respect and self-help, but vulnerable to the massed battalions of power. It was in that same vein that he had devoted such attention to pensions. In *The Great Pensions Swindle*, in 1970, he issued many warnings, won many arguments but failed to bring about a reshaping of policies, as we are now learning to our cost.

Twenty years after the IEA set up shop, in 1979 Margaret Thatcher entered Downing Street to high hopes among her supporters. Unlike the US, where thinktanks – and the IEA was an early example – were brought into administrations favourable to their ideas, the IEA remained strictly outside government.

True, Ralph Harris was elevated to the House of Lords, but

he entered as a crossbencher and remained friendly but critical of the government's achievements. Arthur and his wife Marjorie were particularly keen on the promotion of education vouchers, and had high hopes when Keith Joseph was moved in as secretary of state for education from industry, where the civil servants trampled all over him. They were to be disappointed during Joseph's time at the department, from 1981 to 1986. The IEA won more arguments in theory than in practice, but Seldon kept writing. *Corrigible Capitalism, Incorrigible Socialism* (1980) was followed by *Wither the Welfare State* (1981), *Socialism Explained* (1983), *The New Right Enlightenment* (1985) and *The Riddle of the Voucher* (1986).

His full-time appointment with the IEA ended nearly two decades ago. His *Capitalism* (1990) won the Fisher Prize in 1991, but by that time Thatcher had fallen, and six years after that the Conservative government fell in its turn.

But Tony Blair's incoming Labour government did little to turn the clock back where economic philosophy was concerned. Seldon continued to write for posterity, confident that the worst fallacies were behind, that the Treasury, the Bank of England, the economic ministries and employers' organisations were nearer the mainstream of neo-classical economics than they had been when the IEA had begun its uphill climb in the 1950s of Harold Macmillan and Hugh Gaitskell. If many of Blair's critics in the Labour Party and unions complain that his policies are Thatcherite, they might more accurately describe them as IEA-ite.

The IEA's distance from the Conservative Party, unlike that of the thinktanks of the left, may have appeared disadvantageous during the heyday of Thatcherism, but it was seen as a boon as time went on. IEA scions command several economics faculties in the universities. The IEA remains active and, if not always actually accepted, at least respected and tolerated, and soundly financed.

After his retirement from the directorship Seldon was a consultant and then, finally, in 1990 he became a founder-president and remained one for the rest of of his life. In 2002 he published

The Making of the IEA, and in 2004–05 a collection of his IEA work and material from other sources has been published in seven volumes by the American organisation the Liberty Fund.

Seldon's recreations were cricket, opera, and, as he wrote in *Who's Who*, 'parties for non-conformists'. His house in Kent, 'the Thatched Cottage', is, in spite of its name, quite large, and surrounded by generous gardens. It has always been a centre of conviviality and conversation. In retrospect, it seems that whenever we gathered there for leisured colloquies, the sun always shone.

His personal life was happy and uneventful. He married Marjorie in 1948; she survives him. They had three sons, of whom the youngest, Anthony, has made a name for himself as biographer, educationist and headmaster of an independent school.

The *New York Times*, 15 October 2005

Arthur Seldon, a libertarian economist whose books, pamphlets and articles supplied much of the intellectual artillery that inspired Prime Minister Margaret Thatcher's free-market revolution, died Tuesday at his home in Godden Green in Kent County, England. He was 89.

His death was confirmed by the Institute of Economic Affairs, the research group he helped found and guide.

Long before Mrs Thatcher came to power in 1979 and attacked many decades of ever-increasing government power through privatization and her other free-market policies, intellectuals on the right were formulating novel approaches to education, health and other government services. So initially radical were their notions that *The Independent*, a London newspaper, said this week that they were regarded as 'political crackpots.'

The institute, known by its acronym, IEA, 'plowed a lonely furrow in its espousal of capitalist ideas,' according to Patrick Cosgrave in *Thatcher: The First Term.*

Mrs Thatcher was listening, and regularly lunched at the institute before becoming prime minister, drinking in their message that users, not taxpayers, should pay for government services.

Tony Blair, the current Labour Party prime minister, continued much of Mrs Thatcher's free-market emphasis. She thanked the 'lonely' academics on the 30th anniversary of the institute in 1987, saying, 'They were right and they saved Britain.'

Mr Seldon and Ralph Harris, now Lord Harris, the other founder of the IEA, steered clear of partisan politics, being careful to portray their thoughts as a product of classical liberal economics. They and their colleagues remained strictly outside of government, unlike many of the conservative research groups whose legions streamed into the administrations of President Reagan and subsequent Republicans. They were not even necessarily members of Mrs Thatcher's Conservative Party.

Nor were some of their many ideas for transforming the British welfare state, particularly government vouchers to pay for private schooling, ultimately successful. But the institute helped change the nature of Britain's national conservation, as it also oversaw the proliferation of more than 100 similar institutions to nearly 80 countries.

This effort was greatly aided by Mr Seldon's ability to translate complex economic ideas into clear English. He did this both as an editor of all the institute's publications, more than 350, and as the author of 28 books and some 230 articles.

His trenchant phrasemaking became famous, as in this criticism of socialist economies for providing less choice: 'Socialism is a vast machine for churning out piles of goods marked "Take it or leave it."'

Critics faulted Mr Seldon as seeming to start with an ideological answer he liked and then looking around for a question. In a review of Mr Seldon's 1990 book, *Capitalism*, Gordon Brown, a Labour Party leader who is now chancellor of the exchequer, suggested he made a theology out of free markets.

A letter to *The Times* of London in 1990 attacked Mr Seldon's contention that the spending decisions of people were truer indications of their wishes than elections. The letter writer pointed out that wealthier people have more votes in such a formulation.

Mr Seldon countered such criticisms by advocating a negative income tax, under which the poor would be paid money by the government. He said they could then vote with their money for the services they wanted most.

Arthur Seldon was born in the East End of London on May 29, 1916. His parents died in the flu epidemic of 1918. He was adopted by a childless cobbler and his wife, who, like his parents, were Russian-Jewish immigrants.

In 1934, he won a scholarship to the London School of Economics where he studied with Lionel Robbins and Friedrich Hayek, who taught classical liberal economics. Many others in the school embraced socialism or Communism, with which Mr Seldon briefly flirted.

After graduating with honors, Mr Seldon worked in a

government survey research unit. In 1940, he joined the Army, serving in Africa and Italy. He next taught, edited a trade journal called *Store* and did research for the beer industry.

At *Store*, he met and married Marjorie Perrott. He adopted her son from a previous marriage, and they had two more sons. His survivors were not announced.

In 1957, he became editorial director at the institute, which was set up by businessman Antony Fisher, who had been inspired by a lecture by Mr Hayek. Lord Harris, as general director, handled finances and recruitment.

Mr Seldon co-wrote the first pamphlet of the institute, *Pensions in a Free Society*. It argued for private pensions, something achieved 30 years later. One of his most widely reviewed books was *Capitalism*, which *The Economist* called 'a triumph of the human spirit.'

Mr Seldon liked cricket, opera and having what he called parties for nonconformists at his home, Thatched Cottage, which was quite a large house surrounded by expansive gardens.

Douglas Martin

The Economist, 22 October 2005

'The ideas of economists and political philosophers ... are more powerful than is commonly understood. Indeed, the world is ruled by little else. Madmen in authority, who hear voices in the air, are distilling their frenzy from some academic scribbler of a few years back.' So wrote John Maynard Keynes, the economic architect of the welfare state and the Great Society, and he should have known. But it was Arthur Seldon who took Keynes's words to heart, and paid him back in kind. Mr Seldon marshalled the academic scribblers of his own era to lead the intellectual fight-back against Keynesianism, distilling from free-market economic doctrines ideas that fuelled both the frenzy of Thatcherism and its afterburn, Tony Blair.

The perch from which Mr Seldon directed this campaign was a think-tank, the Institute of Economic Affairs (IEA), which he joined as Editorial Director in 1958. The IEA was founded in 1955 by an old-Etonian chicken farmer called Antony Fisher. Concerned by the waves of nationalisations and economic controls in post-war Britain, Mr Fisher sought advice from the one intellectual who was resisting the tide, an Austrian-born economist, Friedrich von Hayek. Hayek urged him to emulate the Fabian Society, the first socialist think-tank, which had done so much to spread the doctrine of state intervention at the beginning of the century. He should do so, however, from the opposite, free-market point of view.

Fisher's first recruit, as director of the new think-tank, was Ralph Harris, and his second was Mr Seldon. Together they made a formidable team, in place until the mid-1980s, by which time they had moved from the outer fringes to the mainstream of British politics. Mr Harris was the IEA's public face; Mr Seldon, the more thoughtful of the two, was its resident intellectual. A pronounced stutter meant that he seldom spoke in public. But as Editorial Director he oversaw the institute's highly influential publishing programme.

The IEA's pamphlets, modelled on Fabian ones, brought to

the lay reader the ideas of all the leading free-market economists and thinkers of the day. Many of those subjects – reform
of the trade unions, public versus private welfare, the virtues of
floating exchange rates – became the main preoccupations of
the Thatcherites in the 1980s. Mr Seldon's target audience was
what he called the 'second-hand dealers in ideas': journalists,
teachers, academics, businessmen and city analysts who create
the intellectual environment in which politicians have to work.
Mr Seldon's golden rule was that his authors should think of
their subjects regardless of the political context. They were to
expound the verities of economic liberalism and let the politicians come to them, rather than the other way round. It took
quite a long time for this to happen; but eventually, from the
mid-1960s, the politicians began to arrive. As Britain's economic
problems piled up, a trickle of radical Conservatives such as
Enoch Powell, Margaret Thatcher and Geoffrey Howe started
getting involved in the IEA's work, looking for free-market
alternatives.

Mr Seldon, however, kept away from active politics. Having
seen war service in Africa and Italy, he picked a military meta-
phor: the IEA would be the long-range artillery lobbing shells
into enemy lines, 'but it would never be the infantry, engaged in
the short-term face-to-face grappling'. In the mid-1970s, as the
Thatcherite revolution got under way, other think-tanks, such as
the Centre for Policy Studies, were founded to do the
grappling.

A classic liberal

In many ways Mr Seldon was a quintessential Thatcherite, if
never a Conservative. He was born in the East End of London,
to Russian-Jewish immigrants, but lost both parents in the 'flu
epidemic of 1918, when he was three. Adopted by a cobbler,
learning to repair shoes himself, he became a natural and life-
long believer in self-help. He won a state scholarship to the

London School of Economics, where he was inspired to his life's work by Hayek, who was one of his tutors.

Rather than a Tory, Mr Seldon was essentially a classic liberal. Much of his early life was devoted to trying to revive the Gladstonian roots of the Liberal Party, even as it succumbed to the influence of Keynes and others. He always regretted that it was the Conservative Party that took up the IEA's agenda, not the Liberal Party, where his free-market ideas really belonged. This marked him out from most Thatcherites, who, much as they adored economic freedom, often had a Tory dislike of individual liberty in other spheres.

His distance from party politics made him a natural source of wisdom when the next generation of intellectuals came along, in the early 1990s, to try to end the hegemony of Conservatism. Copying Mr Seldon's formula, they started think-tanks such as Demos to create a new intellectual climate that would eventually contribute to Mr Blair's landslide election victory in 1997. Not only had Mr Seldon changed the way that politicians went about their business, establishing the 'battle of ideas' as equal in importance to party politics. Through his tireless campaigning he had also ensured that New Labour would only be taken seriously if it became, essentially, a free-market party as well.

The *Financial Times*, 25 October 2005

Arthur Seldon, who has died at the age of 89, helped to found the free-market Institute of Economic Affairs which became the intellectual progenitor of the Thatcher revolution. Seldon challenged the post-war Keynesian consensus on the welfare state and played a crucial part in creating a centre-right position rooted in economic liberalism. Although not naturally a conservative – he always called himself an old liberal – he had a great influence on Margaret Thatcher and, arguably, on Tony Blair. Many of Thatcher's policies originated in Lord North Street, Westminster, the home of the IEA. On his 80th birthday Baroness Thatcher paid tribute to him for championing free enterprise and the free market. His 'visionary work', she said, had 'inspired much of our success in the 1980s'.

Seldon set up the IEA with Lord Harris of High Cross in 1957 when market economics were unfashionable. From obscurity throughout the 1950s and 1960s, Seldon and a distinguished cadre of writers managed to influence a generation of economists and writers into a fresh way of thinking on the market and on limited government. He also introduced them to such 'foreign' economists as Milton Friedman and Friedrich Hayek, the free market economists who became Nobel Laureates.

Born in 1916 into relative poverty, the son of a Jewish immigrant family in the East End of London, his parents died in the 1918 flu epidemic and he was adopted by a cobbler and his wife. Educated at Raine's Foundation School, he won a scholarship to the London School of Economics where he came under the influence of Hayek, a recently appointed professor. He quickly learnt that almost everything the government does, the market and the private sector could do better. Most important, he realised that, if you want to advance the interests of the working class, capitalism always beats the government. This was the beginning of a life-long campaign against state welfare. From his earliest days he understood that spontaneous working class organisations such as the Friendly Societies provided better health care, old age pensions and unemployment benefit than the vast state bureaucracies that replaced them. Seldon's first paper for the IEA was a stunning piece on the inequities and inefficiencies of the state pension system: a subject that was to bother him all his life. As editorial director, he quickly set about recruiting some of the best names in free market ideas, teaching them how to write clear, concise English.

One of the many reasons for the new right's eventual triumph over the old left was the clarity, as well as the perspicacity, of its arguments. Someone very receptive to Seldon's approach was Milton Friedman, who had a genius for conveying complex ideas in lucid prose, and he led the IEA's onslaught on Keynesianism from the early 1960s. Always anxious to keep his readers up to date with new thinking, Seldon quickly saw the significance of American 'public choice' theory which was emerging in the 1960s. He was a natural anarchist who delighted in offending the welfare establishment. This reached its apogee in 1968 with the publication of *The Price of Blood* which presented the shocking idea that hospital shortages would be solved if blood were bought and sold like any other wanted good. Seldon was a prolific writer. His best work was probably on welfare in which he relentlessly exposed the denial of choice and the dull inefficiency that the state produced in health and pensions.

He and his wife, Marjorie – the couple had three sons – were indefatigable proponents of Friedman's idea of vouchers in education. Perhaps his finest work was the sadly unnoticed book *Capitalism* (1990). Here he celebrated the market system's efficiency but also its contribution to human freedom. He was working to the end – against the state. His seven volume works are being completed by the IEA. Only then will a full evaluation be possible.

Norman Barry

Notes

Introduction

1. Richard Cockett, *Thinking the Unthinkable: Think tanks and the economic counter-revolution, 1931–1983* Fontana Press, London, revised edn, 1995, gives a particularly good account of the evolution of economic ideas in the second half of the twentieth century, putting these changes in the context of earlier ideas and explaining the role of the Institute of Economic Affairs and other think tanks.
2. 'Political power or economic law?', 1914, reprinted in *The Shorter Classics of Böhm-Bawerk*, Libertarian Press, South Holland, IL, 1962.
3. Colin Robinson (ed.), *The Collected Works of Arthur Seldon*, Liberty Fund, Indianapolis, IN, 2005, 7 vols (hereafter *The Collected Works*).
4. Cockett, op. cit., p. 182.
5. All references in the text to Arthur Seldon's publications are to volume and page numbers in *The Collected Works*, op. cit.
6. Chris Tame (1949–2006) founded the Libertarian Alliance and was its director from 1979 to 2006, becoming president in his final year.
7. *Letters on a Birthday: The Unfinished Agenda of Arthur Seldon*, Economic and Literary Books (printed for private circulation), 1996.

8. The authors were approached and their contributions were assembled by John Blundell, Director General of the IEA.

1 Arthur Seldon's early years

1. References to Cecil Margolis in this chapter are to the unpublished autobiographical notes mentioned in the Introduction which were supplied by Philip Margolis, Cecil's eldest son and Arthur's nephew.
2. The addresses are given by Cecil Margolis in his autobiographical notes. Bedford Street was evidently renamed Cavell Street after Nurse Edith Cavell, who helped Allied soldiers escape from occupied Belgium during World War I and was executed by German soldiers in 1915.
3. Ben is said to have been conscripted into the Russian army but escaped and reached Hamburg, from where he worked his passage to London.
4. According to Marjorie Seldon, Arthur's friend was Eric Sharp, who in later life became chairman of Monsanto Chemicals.
5. Seldon recalls this episode in *Capitalism*, in *The Collected Works*, vol. 1, ch. 2, p. 85.
6. Ibid., vol. 1, ch. 2.
7. Peter Seldon believes that his grandmother may have called herself 'Mrs Marks' even during her marriage to Marks Slaberdain, finding the name 'Slaberdain' rather unwieldy. Private communication from Peter Seldon, September 2008.
8. In *Capitalism*, in *The Collected Works*, vol. 1, p. 86, Seldon says that the Board of Guardians supplied 'eight shillings' worth of groceries in a stout paper bag'. Given what is known about the Jewish voluntary aid societies at the time, however, it may be that the source of the help was one of

the 'Chevras'. For an explanation of the system of voluntary aid in the Jewish community in the late nineteenth century, see Chapter 3.

9. Arthur's stepfather died in 1936. See *Capitalism*, in *The Collected Works*, vol. 1, p. 94.

10. An article by Seldon on the influence of Cannan, published in *Economic Affairs*, appears in vol. 7 of *The Collected Works*, pp 69–75. Seldon was very critical of the state of the LSE at the time he was writing. After explaining Cannan's influence, he says, *inter alia*, that 'Cannan would now see tracts of intellectual desert over the Houghton Street buildings of the LSE in the 1990s'. See also Cockett, op. cit., pp 25–35, on the LSE economists of the 1930s and the influence of Cannan.

11. Seldon's fellow student, Arthur (later Sir Arthur) Lewis, was also awarded the Nobel Economics Prize.

12. For example, *Prices and Production*, 1931, *Monetary Theory and the Trade Cycle*, 1933, and *Collectivist Economic Planning*.

13. *The Collected Works*, vol. 7, p. 34.

14. Some are collected in *Essays on Economics and Economists*, University of Chicago Press, 1994, and *The Firm, the Market and the Law*, University of Chicago Press, 1998.

15. For example, Lionel Robbins, *The Great Depression*, Macmillan, London, 1934, p. 194.

16. Lionel Robbins, *An Essay on the Nature and Significance of Economic Science*, Macmillan, 1932.

17. *The Collected Works*, vol. 3, p. 568.

18. Arnold Plant, 'The economics of the native question', *Voorslag*, Durban, May–July 1927, reprinted in *Selected Essays and Addresses of Arnold Plant*, Routledge and Kegan Paul, London and New York, 1974, p. 4.

19. For example, 'The economic theory concerning patents for inventions', *Economica*, February 1934, and 'The economic aspect of copyright in books', *Economica*, May 1934. Both are reprinted in *Selected Essays*, op. cit.

20. 'Political power or economic law?', op. cit.

21. *The Collected Works*, vol. 5, p. 19.

22. Ibid., p. 193.

23. 'Political power or economic law', op. cit.

24. The change of name was made on 1 August 1939 (see page 156). Presumably, Plant's concern was that, at a time when Jews were being persecuted in Germany and anti-Semitism was quite common in other countries, a Jewish-sounding name might be a handicap. Two years previously, on 28 September 1937, Seldon had changed his first name to Arthur from Abraham.

25. Tame notes that Tiptaft was not a consistent classical liberal and produced a number of papers that favoured planning. He published his autobiography in 1954: *The Individualist*, Norman Tiptaft, Birmingham, 1954.

26. '1944–1945', *Valjean Times*, 30 December, 1944, 2(4).

27. According to Cecil Margolis, it was poliomyelitis which Seldon contracted.

28. Where Mrs Marks lived for part of the war, with the family of Arthur's brother, Cecil, to be 'away from the bombs', according to Cecil Margolis.

29. Marjorie's father, Wilfred, was Mentioned in Dispatches in 1915 for his attempt to rescue a colleague. He was crippled and lost the use of his right arm and was thus unable to complete his medical studies. Private communication from Marjorie Seldon, 29 July 2008.

30. Marjorie recalls that she went to South Africa early in 1939 when she was nineteen and helped her cousin Betty (wife of George Sachs, a surgeon at Groote Schuur Hospital in Cape Town) write some left-wing newspaper articles in the weekly, *The Guardian*, that Betty published. Marjorie returned home in late 1939 on the *Union Castle* – a perilous journey given that U-boats were at that time passing through the Western Approaches. Private communication from Marjorie Seldon, 29 July 2008.

31. Rt Hon. Isaac Foot (1880–1960), *Liberty and the Liberal Heritage*, Ramsay Muir Memorial Lecture 1947, Victor Gollancz, London, 1948.

2 The LSE and the early war years: some reflections by contemporaries

1. For example, *Capitalism*, in *The Collected Works*, vol. 1, ch. 2.
2. *The Collected Works*, vol. 7, p. 75.
3. Ibid., p. 34.

3 The effects of Arthur Seldon's upbringing

1. Jonathan Sacks, *Morals and Markets*, Occasional Paper 108, IEA, London, 1999, pp. 18–19.
2. Beatrice Potter, 'The Jewish community', in Charles Booth, *Life and Labour of the People of London*, London, 1889, pp. 564–90.
3. Ibid., p. 564.
4. Ibid., p. 567.
5. Ibid., p. 567.
6. As explained in Chapter 1, it is possible the Slaberdain family received help from one of these Chevras when Seldon's stepfather died in 1926. See Chapter 1, note 8.
7. 'The Jewish community', op. cit., p. 570.
8. The total Jewish population of the area was estimated to be 60,000 to 70,000, of which about half had been born abroad; ibid., p. 577.
9. Ibid., p. 571.
10. Ibid., p. 573.
11. Ibid., p. 574.
12. Ibid., p. 586.

13. Ibid., p. 589.
14. Ibid., p. 590.
15. Gertrude Himmelfarb, *The Demoralization of Society: From Victorian Virtues to Modern Values*, Choice in Welfare Series 22, IEA, London, 1995, pp. 170–87.
16. Ibid., p. 186.
17. Interview with Gertrude Himmelfarb, 'Learning from Victorian virtues', *Religion and Liberty*, 5(4), July/August 1995.
18. See, for example, 'Envoi: a promise kept', in *Capitalism*, in *The Collected Works*, vol. 1, pp. 435–6.

4 Seldon's move to the IEA: a turning point in life

1. There are references to these articles and, more generally, to Seldon's work with Tedder in *Capitalism*, in *The Collected Works*, vol. 1, pp. 98–101.
2. Antony Fisher, *Must History Repeat Itself?*, Churchill Press, London, 1974. The Hayek/Fisher meeting and its consequences are discussed in Gerald Frost, *Antony Fisher: Champion of Liberty*, Profile Books, London, 2002, chs 3, 4 and 5, and in John Blundell, 'Introduction' to *The Road to Serfdom*, Occasional Paper 136, IEA, London, pp. 27–9.
3. *The Intellectuals and Socialism*, Rediscovered Riches no. 4, IEA, London, 1998.
4. The trust deed founding the IEA was signed in November 1955 by the three founding trustees, Fisher, Oliver Smedley and J. S. Harding, but Fisher broke with the others soon after the founding. The story of the founding of the IEA is told in Frost, *Antony Fisher: Champion of Liberty*, op. cit. (see especially ch. 5); in John Blundell, *Waging the War of Ideas*, Occasional Paper 131, IEA, London, 2nd edn, 2003; and in Cockett, op. cit., ch. 4.

5. There is an excellent account of Fisher's life in *Antony Fisher: Champion of Liberty*, op. cit. His work in founding think tanks around the world is discussed in ch. 8 of that book. See also Cockett, op. cit., pp. 306–308.

6. *The Collected Works*, vol. 2, ch. 1.

7. Seldon's original introduction into Liberal Party circles occurred when he joined the LSE Liberal Society in his student days, because 'The Conservatives were too socialist'; *Capitalism*, in *The Collected Works*, vol. 1, p. 94.

8. *The Collected Works*, vol. 2, ch. 2, and John Meadowcroft and Jaime Reynolds, 'Liberals and the New Right', *Journal of Liberal History*, 47, Summer 2005.

9. Meadowcroft and Reynolds, op. cit.

10. Ibid.

11. *The Collected Works*, vol. 1, Introduction, p. x.

12. *Pensions in a Free Society*, IEA, London, 1957.

13. Letter from Mrs Heather Owen (née Grange) to Marjorie Seldon, dated 2 February 2008.

14. Arthur Seldon, 'From the LSE to the IEA', *The Collected Works*, vol. 7, pp. 69–75.

15. See, for instance, 'Living with Arthur', in Colin Robinson (ed.), *Ralph Harris in His Own Words*, Edward Elgar, Cheltenham and Northampton, MA, 2008.

16. Discussed, for instance, in 'Living with Arthur', op. cit.; Ralph Harris and Arthur Seldon, *A Conversation with Harris and Seldon*, Occasional Paper 116, IEA, London, 2001: *The Collected Works*, vol. 1, General Introduction; John Blundell *Waging the War of Ideas*, op. cit.; and Cockett, op. cit., ch. 4.

17. *The Collected Works*, vol. 1, Introduction.

18. Ralph Harris and Arthur Seldon, *Not from Benevolence … 20 Years of Economic Dissent*, Hobart Paperback Special, IEA, London, 1977, p. 124.

19. Thomas Kuhn, *The Structure of Scientific Revolutions*, University of Chicago Press, Chicago, IL, 1962.

20. J. K. Galbraith, *The Affluent Society*, Mentor Books, 1958. The quotations are from ch. II.

21. A prime example of the conventional wisdom of the early 21st century is the view that damaging climate change is under way and can be countered only by drastic centralised action. See, for example, Colin Robinson, 'Economics, politics and climate change: are the sceptics right?', Julian Hodge Bank Lecture 2008, Julian Hodge Bank and Cardiff Business School, Cardiff.
22. See Chapter 1.
23. Milton Friedman, 'The IEA's influence in our times', in *A Conversation with Harris and Seldon*, op. cit., p. 70.
24. 'Living with Arthur', op. cit.
25. Ibid., p. 14.

5 Arthur Seldon's role in the IEA

1. *The Collected Works*, vol. 1, General Introduction.
2. 'Living with Arthur', op. cit.
3. *The Collected Works*, vol. 1, General Introduction. John Blundell recalls that Antony Fisher told him that the concept of a series was his idea. Personal communication from John Blundell, October 2008.
4. Some of Seldon's prefaces are reprinted in *The Collected Works*, vol. 7.
5. Cockett, op. cit.
6. Ibid., ch. 3.
7. Milton Friedman, *The Counter-Revolution in Monetary Theory*, Occasional Paper 33, IEA, London, 1970.
8. *Letters on a Birthday*, op. cit., includes many tributes to Arthur's editorial skills.
9. Gordon Tullock, Introduction, *The Vote Motive*, Hobart Paperback 33, IEA, London, revised edn 2006 (first published 1976 as Hobart Paperback 9).
10. See Ralph Harris, Tribute, in Appendix 3.
11. Cockett, op. cit., pp. 143–5.

12. Private communication from Ralph Harris, 6 September 2006.

13. Private communication from Marjorie Seldon, 12 July 2008.

14. Michael Cooper and Anthony Culyer, *The Price of Blood*, Hobart Paper 41, IEA, London, 1968.

15. Seldon describes his hospital experience and the commissioning of the paper in *Capitalism*, in *The Collected Works*, vol. 1, pp. 369–70.

16. *The Collected Works*, vol. 7, p. 231.

6 The Harris–Seldon partnership: working together and its problems

1. *Ralph Harris in His Own Words*, op. cit., p. 17.

2. Ibid., p. 16.

3. Ibid., p. 7.

4. Robert Miller and John B. Wood, *What Price Unemployment?*, Hobart Paper 92, IEA, London, 1982, and *Exchange Control for Ever?*, Research Monograph 33, IEA, London, 1979.

5. *Ralph Harris in His Own Words*, op. cit., p. 14.

6. It is not absolutely clear that Ralph Harris was given his peerage for his IEA work, because he also wrote speeches for Margaret Thatcher. Personal communication from John Blundell, October 2008.

7. *Ralph Harris in His Own Words*, op. cit., p. 16.

8. Ibid., p. 14.

9. Ibid., pp. 14–15.

10. Ibid., p. 15.

11. He retired from full-time work in 1981 at the age of 65, but remained at the Institute in an advisory capacity until 1988, later becoming, with Harris, a founder-president.

12. *A Conversation with Harris and Seldon*, op. cit., p. 35.

7 Family life

1. See *Charge, The Collected Works*, vol. 4, pp. 278–80, and *The Riddle of the Voucher, The Collected Works*, vol. 4, pp. 319–417.
2. Arthur Seldon, *Prime Mover of Progress: The entrepreneur in capitalism and socialism*, Readings 23, IEA, London, 1980.
3. When Seldon looked back on his time at the IEA, he used a cricketing analogy to explain what he had tried to do, which was 'putting the best players in to bat'. See Chapter 5.
4. He has written or edited over twenty-five books. His most recent is *Blair Unbound*, Simon and Schuster, 2007.

8 Working with Arthur Seldon

1. Hobart Paperback 21, IEA, London, 1986. *The Collected Works*, vol. 4, pp. 319–417.
2. Sir Keith Joseph (1918–94), Secretary of State for Education and Science from 1981 until 1986. The extent to which the civil servants ruled the roost was illustrated for me by an unannounced visit from Sir Keith to the IEA, when he asked whether I could help him make a photocopy, on the machine in the IEA library, of a document that he didn't want his staff to see because they wouldn't agree with it – this, from a member of the Cabinet.
3. A classic illustration of the difference between the two men occurred during a lunchtime visit of Mrs Thatcher to the IEA in the mid-1980s. She had recently permitted Mercury a limited degree of competition with British Telecom in a small handful of markets, thus increasing the number of people with a direct interest in opposing genuine liberalisation, and one of my colleagues, John Burton, made no bones about pointing out the error of that policy. Mrs Thatcher wasn't used to being talked to so bluntly, and

bridled. 'Never mind all that,' said Ralph, keen to preserve harmony around the table: 'Let's drink a toast to the best prime minister since Churchill.' Arthur raised his glass and said, in a stage whisper: 'I'll take a sip.'

4. One particular moment of that week is worth preserving. The format of a full, week-long Mont Pelerin meeting is generally two days of papers at either end, with a breather on the Wednesday for an outing to local points of interest. On this occasion the day out ended with a visit to Pitlochry, to attend a performance of James Bridie's *The Forrigan Reel*. Pitlochry Festival Theatre was then little more than a large tent, capable of holding 500, 400 or so of whom were MPS members and their wives or husbands, who had already had two solid days of papers on the contemporary relevance of Adam Smith. So when the heroine of the play complained that she felt unwell, as if 'her heart were being crushed by a great invisible hand', the gale of helpless laughter which followed lasted so long that it held up the action.

5. 'The necessity of unemployment', *Economic Affairs*, vol. 2, no. 4, July 1982, pp. 194–6.

6. In Richard C. Stapleton, 'Why Recession Benefits Britain', *Economic Affairs*, vol. 2, no. 1, October 1981, pp. 7–11.

7. F. A. Hayek, 'Two pages of fiction: the impossibility of socialist calculation', *Economic Affairs*, vol. 2, no. 3, April 1982, pp. 135–42.

9 An overview

1. *The Collected Works*, vol. 1, General Introduction.

2. *The Collected Works*, vol. 3, Introduction, p x. Pennance checked the manuscript before publication but died before the second edition was published. Anthony Seldon recalls how upset his father was at his friend's death.

3. Other examples are in vol. 3 of *The Collected Works*. See Introduction, pp. xii–xv.

4. Ibid., p. 130.

5. Ibid., Introduction, p. xv.

6. *The Collected Works*, vol. 7, p. 83.

7. *Corrigible Capitalism, Incorrigible Socialism*, Occasional Paper 57, IEA, London, 1980.

8. *The Collected Works*, vol. 2.

9. Mark Blaug, 'Classical economics', in John Eatwell, Murray Milgate and Peter Newman (eds), *The New Palgrave – A Dictionary of Economics*, Macmillan, London, New York and Tokyo, 1987.

10. F. A. Hayek, 'The meaning of competition', in *Individualism and Economic Order*, George Routledge, London, 1948.

11. See Chapter 4 above and *The Collected Works*, vol. 7, pp. 34 and 84, and the Introduction, pp. ix–x.

12. See, for instance, *Denationalisation of Money*, IEA, London, 1990, in which Hayek acknowledges Seldon's help with that and with earlier IEA publications of his. Seldon's 'beneficial care has already made much more readable some of my shorter essays published by that Institute'. *The Collected Works*, vol. 7, Introduction, p. xiii.

13. Arthur Seldon, *The Dilemma of Democracy*, in *The Collected Works*, vol. 5, p. 85.

14. Cockett, op. cit., pp. 150–55.

10 The virtues of capitalism

1. *The Collected Works*, vol. 1, p. 13.

2. *The Collected Works*, vol. 7, pp. 279–80.

3. A condensed version of *Capitalism* was published by the IEA in 2007 as Occasional Paper 140.

11 The problem of over-government

1. Alan Peacock, *Public Choice Analysis in Historical Perspective*, Cambridge University Press, Cambridge, New York and Melbourne, 1992.
2. Anthony Downs, *An Economic Theory of Democracy*, Harper and Row, New York, 1957.
3. Another early seminal contribution was by Duncan Black, *The Theory of Committees and Elections*, Cambridge University Press, Cambridge, 1958.
4. Harry G. Johnson, *The Economic Approach to Social Questions*, Weidenfeld and Nicolson, London, 1967, p. 16.
5. John Blundell and Colin Robinson, 'Gordon Tullock and the IEA: bridging the Atlantic', Institute of Economic Affairs, http://publicchoice.info/TullockTales/JBlundellt. pdf.
6. *The Collected Works*, vol. 1, General Introduction, p. xiii.
7. *The Economics of Politics*, IEA, London, 1978.
8. John Blundell recalls that Tullock once said that '*The Vote Motive* did more to spread public understanding of Public Choice than any other single publication'. Private communication from John Blundell, October 2008.
9. Peter Kurrild-Klitgaard, 'Editor's Introduction', *The Vote Motive*, op. cit., p. 16.
10. Blundell and Robinson, op. cit.
11. *The Collected Works*, vol. 5, pp. 3–19.
12. Ibid., pp. 23–47.
13. Ibid., pp. 71–146.
14. Ibid.; Seldon's contribution is pp. 149–90.
15. Ibid., pp. 193–6.

12 The perils of the welfare state

1. *A Conversation with Harris and Seldon*, op. cit., p. 28.

2. Ibid., p. 51.

3. IEA Archive, quoted in Cockett, op. cit., p. 138.

4. *The Collected Works*, vol. 6, p. 68.

5. 'The reluctant crutch', *The Collected Works*, vol. 6, pp. 3–5.

6. For instance, see *Pensions for Prosperity*, in *The Collected Works*, vol. 6, p. 11.

7. *The Collected Works*, vol. 6, p. 47.

8. Ibid., p. 59.

9. Ibid., pp. 51–63.

10. Ibid., p. 72.

11. Ibid., p. 95.

12. Ibid., pp. 105–222.

13. Ibid., p. 237.

14. Ibid., pp. 225–66.

15. Ibid., pp. 269–85.

16. Ibid., p. 303.

17. *The Collected Works*, vol. 4, p. 286.

18. Ibid., pp. 303–18.

19. Ibid., pp. 319–416.

Bibliography

(no editor named) (1996), *Letters on a Birthday: The Unfinished Agenda of Arthur Seldon*, Economic and Literary Books (printed for private circulation).

Black, Duncan (1958), *The Theory of Committees and Elections*, Cambridge: Cambridge University Press.

Blundell, John (2003) *Waging the War of Ideas*, 2nd edn, Occasional Paper 131, London: IEA.

Blundell, John and Colin Robinson (n.d.), 'Gordon Tullock and the IEA: bridging the Atlantic', London: IEA, http://publicchoice.info/TullockTales/JBlundellt.pdf.

Böhm-Bawerk, Eugen von (1962 [1914]), 'Political power or economic law?', reprinted in *The Shorter Classics of Bohm-Bawerk*, South Holland, IL: Libertarian Press.

Coase, Ronald (1994), *Essays on Economics and Economists*, Chicago, IL: University of Chicago Press.

Coase, Ronald (1998), *The Firm, the Market and the Law*, Chicago, IL: University of Chicago Press.

Cockett, Richard (1995), *Thinking the Unthinkable: Think tanks and the economic counter-revolution, 1931–1983*, revised edn, London: Fontana Press.

Cooper, Michael and Anthony Culyer (1968), *The Price of Blood*, Hobart Paper 41, London: IEA.

Downs, Anthony (1957), *An Economic Theory of Democracy*, New York: Harper and Row.

Eatwell, John, Murray Milgate and Peter Newman (eds) (1987), *The New Palgrave – A Dictionary of Economics*, London, New York and Tokyo: Macmillan.

Fisher, Antony (1974), *Must History Repeat Itself?*, London: Churchill Press.

Foot, Rt Hon. Isaac (1948), *Liberty and the Liberal Heritage*, Ramsay Muir Memorial Lecture 1947, London: Victor Gollancz.

Friedman, Milton (1970), *The Counter-Revolution in Monetary Theory*, Occasional Paper 33, London: IEA.

Frost, Gerald (2002), *Antony Fisher: Champion of Liberty*, London: Profile Books.

Galbraith, J. K. (1958), *The Affluent Society*, Mentor Books.

Harris, Ralph and Arthur Seldon (2001), *A Conversation with Harris and Seldon*, Occasional Paper 116, London: IEA.

Hayek, Friedrich (1948), *Individualism and Economic Order*, London: George Routledge.

Hayek, Friedrich (3rd edn, 1990), *Denationalisation of Money*, London: IEA.

Hayek, Friedrich (1998), *The Intellectuals and Socialism*, Rediscovered Riches 4, London: IEA.

Himmelfarb, Gertrude (1995), *The Demoralization of Society: From Victorian Virtues to Modern Values*, Choice in Welfare Series 22, London: IEA.

Johnson, Harry G. (1967), *The Economic Approach to Social Questions*, London: Weidenfeld and Nicolson.

Meadowcroft, John and Jaime Reynolds (2005), 'Liberals and the New Right', *Journal of Liberal History*, 47.

Miller, Robert and John B. Wood (1979), *Exchange Control for Ever?*, Research Monograph 33, London: IEA.

Miller, Robert and John B. Wood (1982), *What Price Unemployment?*, Hobart Paper 92, London: IEA.

Peacock, Alan (1992), *Public Choice Analysis in Historical Perspective*, Cambridge, New York and Melbourne: Cambridge University Press.

Plant, Arnold (1974), *Selected Essays and Addresses of Arnold Plant*, London and New York: Routledge and Kegan Paul.

Potter, Beatrice (1889), 'The Jewish community', in Charles
    Booth, *Life and Labour of the People of London*, London, pp.
    564–90.
Robbins, Lionel (1932), *An Essay on the Nature and Significance
    of Economic Science*, London: Macmillan.
Robbins, Lionel (1934), *The Great Depression*, London:
    Macmillan.
Robinson, Colin (ed.) (2005), *The Collected Works of Arthur
    Seldon*, 7 vols, Indianapolis: Liberty Fund.
Robinson, Colin (2008), 'Economics, politics and climate
    change: are the sceptics right?', Julian Hodge Bank Lecture,
    Julian Hodge Bank and Cardiff Business School, Cardiff.
Robinson, Colin (ed.) (2008), *Ralph Harris in His Own Words*,
    Cheltenham and Northampton, MA: Edward Elgar.
Sacks, Jonathan (1999), *Morals and Markets*, Occasional Paper
    108, London: IEA.
Seldon, Anthony (2007), *Blair Unbound*, London: Simon and
    Schuster.
Seldon, Arthur (1980a), *Prime Mover of Progress: The entrepreneur
    in capitalism and socialism*, Readings 23, London: IEA.
Seldon, Arthur (1980b), *Corrigible Capitalism, Incorrigible
    Socialism*, Occasional Paper 57, London: IEA.
Seldon, Arthur (1986), *The Riddle of the Voucher*, Hobart
    Paperback 21, London: IEA.
Tiptaft, Norman (1954), *The Individualist*, Birmingham.

About the contributors

Martin Anderson worked at the Institute of Economic Affairs from 1977 until 1987, working mainly on *Economic Affairs* and eventually becoming its editor. He then worked at the Organisation for Economic Cooperation and Development in Paris for ten years (1987–97), where he edited the English-language edition of the *OECD Observer*, with special responsibility for its statistical supplement, 'The OECD in Figures'. Based back in London since 1997, he writes freelance about classical music for a variety of publications, publishes books on music as Toccata Press and runs his own CD label, Toccata Classics, which specialises in releasing recordings of neglected music.

Patrick Minford has been Professor of Applied Economics at the Cardiff Business School, University of Wales at Cardiff, since October 1997. From 1976 to 1997 he was Professor of Applied Economics at Liverpool University. He was a member of the Monopolies and Mergers Commission from 1990 to 1996 and one of HM Treasury's Panel of Forecasters (the 'Six Wise Men') from January 1993 to December 1996. He was awarded the CBE for services to economics in 1996. He is the author of books and articles on exchange rates, unemployment, housing and macroeconomics.

Colin Robinson has been Professor of Economics (now Emeritus) at the University of Surrey since 1968. His research and writings have been mainly in energy economics and utility regulation. He edited *The Collected Works of Arthur Seldon* (seven volumes) in 2005. In 1998 he received from the International Association for Energy Economics its 'Outstanding Contribution to the Profession and its Literature' award. From 1992 to 2002 he was Editorial Director of the Institute of Economic Affairs, in addition to his university post.

Stuart Waterhouse graduated from LSE with first class honours in 1939 and then served in the army for six years, two of which he spent on Field Marshal Montgomery's staff, where he rose to the rank of lieutenant-colonel. On leaving the army he took up the London University Cassel Travelling Scholarship that had been awarded to him in 1939 and went to the USA to study marketing strategy. He then had a varied business career, including being marketing director of an advertising agency and a financial consultant.

Basil Yamey, who was best man at Arthur Seldon's wedding in 1948, joined the staff of the London School of Economics in 1947 and was appointed Professor of Economics at LSE in 1960. Also in 1960 he wrote the first Hobart Paper for the Institute of Economic Affairs, on resale price maintenance, widely regarded as very influential in abolition of the practice. He has written on the economics of retailing, on industrial structure, on monopoly and restrictive practices, on commodity markets, on the economics of developing countries and on the history of accounting.

Index